WHO OWNS STONEHENGE?

WHO OWNS STONEHENGE?

CHRISTOPHER CHIPPINDALE

PAUL DEVEREUX

PETER FOWLER

RHYS JONES

TIM SEBASTIAN

B. T. Batsford Ltd, London

This book is for Stonehenge.

Typeset by Servis Filmsetting Ltd, Manchester
and printed in Great Britain by
Butler and Tanner, Frome, Somerset
for the Publishers B.T. Batsford Ltd
4 Fitzhardinge Street, London W1H OAH
ISBN 0 7134 6455 0

ACKNOWLEDGEMENTS

We are grateful to the organizers of the World Archaeological Congress, in particular Professor Peter Ucko, whose invitation to debate Stonehenge first brought us together as a group; we thank Tim Malyon for his participation in that beginning.

We acknowledge with thanks permission to quote from the National Council for Civil Liberties' publication, *Stonehenge: a report into the civil liberties implications of the events relating to the convoys of summer 1985 and 1986* (1986).

Frontispiece A favourite of ours among the Stonehenge stones is the sarsen upright whose natural markings make the shape of a face.
Photograph by Mick Sharp.

CONTENTS

CONTRIBUTORS

Christopher Chippindale is an academic archaeologist whose work mostly concerns the rock-art of Alpine Europe and formal mathematical approaches to art and artefacts. He also works on the history of ideas about the past, and wrote *Stonehenge complete* (1983) as a full-length account of how one monument has been seen and understood since earliest modern times. From 1985 to 1988 he was research fellow in archaeology at Girton College, Cambridge; since 1987 he has edited the journal *Antiquity*, and since 1988 he has been assistant curator for later archaeology in the Cambridge University Museum of Archaeology and Anthropology.

Paul Devereux has researched into leys and associated geomantic subjects for nearly 20 years. Editor of the *Ley Hunter* since 1976, he is also the founder and director of the Dragon Project Trust, an investigation into unusual energies at prehistoric sites. He is author of *Earthlights* and (with Ian Thomson) of the classic *Ley Hunter's Companion*. Among his recent books are *Lines on the Landscape* (with Nigel Pennick), *Earth Lights Revelation* and *Places of Power*. A director of the Centre for Earth Mysteries Studies, he lectures and researches widely on controversial aspects of archaeology in Britain and the USA, and in Europe. He lives in Penzance.

Peter Fowler is Professor of Archaeology at the University of Newcastle upon Tyne where he is head of the Department of Archaeology and Keeper of the Museum of Antiquities and teaches a course entitled 'Heritage, Management and Society'. He was formerly Reader in Archaeology at the University of Bristol and Secretary to the Royal Commission on the Historical Monuments of England. His main academic interests are in the archaeology of landscapes and of farming, the methodologies and practice of fieldwork, and the role of the past in the present. He lectures widely and has variously been author of or editor and contributor to many books and journals including *The Farming of Prehistoric Britain* (1983) and *Images of Prehistory* (1990). Involved in 'public archaeology' throughout his career, he has enjoyed a long association with radio and television; he is currently an elected member of the Council of the National Trust, on its Executive and Properties Committees and chairman of its Archaeology Panel, and archaeological consultant to the Forestry Commission.

Rhys Jones is Senior Fellow in the Research School of Pacific Studies at the Australian National University in Canberra. Welsh by upbringing and a speaker of Welsh, he has been particularly interested in the place of the past in the Welsh and in the Australian peoples' vision of themselves. Many of his professional studies have concerned the early settlement of Australia. Among his fieldwork has been a major survey of Kakadu, in the tropical north of Australia, where his fieldwork in archaeology and rock-art was influential in the creating of Kakadu National Park, and the discoveries of cave sites in Tasmania that proved that the island was settled in Pleistocene times. He is a member of the Gorsedd of the National Eisteddfod of Wales.

Tim Sebastian is the Secular Arch-Druid.

PREFACE

A decade ago the answer to the question, 'Who owns Stonehenge?' required only two sentences. Physically, Stonehenge belonged to the nation, that is, to the Department of the Environment, as the agency of the British government concerned with ancient monuments. Intellectually, it belonged to the archaeologists, as the experts in these matters. The story is more complicated now, sufficiently so that a proper answer to the questions takes this small book.

The origin of this book, and the bringing-together between one set of covers of these contributors, lie in a discussion about Stonehenge at the World Archaeological Congress held at Southampton as long ago as 1986. One concern of the Congress was to explore the variety of views in which the past can be seen. We looked especially at the way in which archaeology – like any academic discipline that changes how people see the world and their place in it – has political aspects. These are most evident outside Europe, in countries like Australia and the Americas where the displacement of aboriginal peoples by European immigrants in, by archaeological standards, very recent times has brought their history and archaeology into contention. There, increasing and increasingly polarized divergences of interest between natives and newcomers are becoming apparent.

The Australian bicentennial early in 1988 commemorated both the 200th anniversary of European settlement there, and the taking of the continent by the colonists from those who had been living there, as archaeologists now know, upwards of 30,000 years. 'Who owns the Australian past?' is now an uncomfortable question, and it begins to become, 'Who ought to own Australia?' 'Who owns the American past?' will be a common and an uncomfortable question in 1992, the 500th anniversary of the European discovery of the New World and its first taking from its aborigines. That New World was, of course, only 'New' to we Europeans who had chanced to be ignorant of it.

In Europe, suffering no such immigrations and dispossessions in modern times, the issues have not often arisen directly. Stonehenge is an exception, where opposed views and varied moral or spiritual land-claims to the place have been clear, public and even violent. At the Southampton congress we spoke about owning Stonehenge, within the larger framework of the question, 'Who owns the past?'

Some things have changed since, so this is the Stonehenge that we see in 1990. The first chapter lays out the issues and their context, both as to the physical Stonehenge and as to the intellectual history of the place and claims to it. The next four chapters give views of Stonehenge as it is seen from four directions. The next chapter summarizes the story of Stonehenge and the 'Convoy', an odd business

1 Stonehenge is a deserved favourite among cartoonists' subjects – whatever the joke is really about.
Drawing by Merrilee Harpur.

about Stonehenge in a free society which we think is too important to be forgotten as a passing curiosity. Finally we look to Stonehenge tomorrow, finding some common ground that is founded in a common interest, for all of us are people in whose lives the grandest relic of the aboriginal British has a special place.

All of us, involved in one way or another, would record our profound relief that the appalling scenes associated with Stonehenge in 1985 and 1986 have not been repeated. 'Is Stonehenge worth it?' was a question we were all asked, and asked ourselves. At one level, the answer has to be, 'No'; but, at another, and more strongly, it has to be, 'Yes', if only because the Stonehenge issue was not only about Stonehenge. For decades now, events at Stonehenge have contrived to reflect in miniature the changing spirit of the larger society in which it stands. What we see in this mirror for our times is about ourselves, all of us, including you – our past and our present and, some would say, our future too.

CHAPTER ONE

THE
STONEHENGE
PHENOMENON

Christopher Chippindale

'Stonehenge' is the name of an archaeological site, the one name of a British prehistoric site that everyone in Britain knows, and one of the few ancient places which is famous across the world. But to call it an 'archaeological site' is only part of the essence; for while it is undoubtedly that, it is also much more.

The site, the name, and the things they stand for form overlapping layers of meaning, of significance and symbolism, which themselves have a long history; it is eight hundred years at least since the 'modern' response to Stonehenge made itself heard. Beneath its weathered old surface, a superficially straightforward site is just one item in a compound of powerful ingredients: archaeology, yes, and landscape history, but, overpowering the delicacies of scholarship, a stronger and bubbling brew of issues concerning intellectual freedom, rational and intuitive knowledge, preservation, presentation and access, the place and role of religious beliefs, the State and its dissidents, the rights of dispossessed ethnic minorities, and even the concept of ownership. It is no answer to say that Stonehenge is part of the 'national heritage' (it is protected as a monument 'of national importance'), or even the 'international heritage' (it has been declared an official 'World Heritage Site'). 'Who owns the past?' becomes, when you think about it, 'Who owns the what?' In the case of 'Who owns Stonehenge?', a whole variety of present and past visions are encapsulated in the physical place.

Our aim is at least to ask the question. Some things have been done to, about and in the name of Stonehenge, particularly in the 1980s, which seem to stem from assumptions that deserve exposure and examination. The site's aura has been recently burnished – or tarnished – by detailed and percipient archaeological work, by a revival of its role as a pagan religious focus, and by its popularity as a place to visit, probably for as many personal reasons as there are visitors.

Stonehenge may be 4000 and more years old, but it is an epitome of Britain in the later twentieth century. It is truly a monument of *our* age, as it has made itself into a contemporary place for past ages: to study Stonehenge is to be a student of current affairs. We suspect it has always been thus and, in writing and editing this book together, as a self-conscious tract for our own times, we sense that we are continuing a tradition that may originate long before the earliest surviving written references in Norman England.

The authors of this book certainly do not own Stonehenge, as writers, earth-mystery researchers, Welshmen, Druids or archaeologists, or as citizens of the United Kingdom or of a 'global village': our position is of tolerance, of attempts to understand the other Stonehenges that have been made, as well as the one each of us has made for himself.

In the western world that we all inhabit, the secure title of legal ownership, with its rights and responsibilities, is a central social concept: hence 'Who *owns*?' is the question that presents and that may resolve conflict. The present physical state of Stonehenge is the product of ownership: people, organizations have done things to it because they owned it in the legal sense, or because they had a 'proper' interest. But is this the right question? – is *ownership* the point at all. The very concept of proprietorship is one of our own culture. The Victorian gentleman who was the legal 'owner' of Stonehenge proudly called himself its 'proprietor'. We do not know what concepts of law, of ownership or of proprietorship the builders of Stonehenge had. It may well not have been 'owned' in our sense at all, and its subsequent accretions of wide-ranging and incompatible symbolisms, with their partial claims, may all be 'illegitimate' to any common sense its builder had. Perhaps no one did, can or should try to own it.

We shall see.

WHAT STONEHENGE IS

First, what is Stonehenge? What is there to own?

Stonehenge is the ruin of an ancient stone structure, now known to be some 4000 years old (fig. 2). It stands on open downland 3 km (2 miles) west of the little town of Amesbury, Wiltshire, in southern England (fig. 3).

On the ground, Stonehenge can seem a confusion of stones, standing and lying, whole and broken. Some stones implied in its very regular design are missing, taken away later or never set in place. But the basic plan is straightforward enough (fig. 4). From the outside working in, the central stone setting has:

– an *outer circle* of neatly trimmed upright stones, an average 4 m (13 ft) above
   ground, about 2 m (6.5 ft) wide and 1 m (3 ft) thick, and standing about 1 $\frac{1}{2}$ m
   (5 ft) apart. These are *sarsens*, a very hard variety of sandstone which is now
   mainly found in north Wiltshire. The circle, of about 33 m (108 ft) diameter,
   needed 30 uprights altogether. Set on top of the uprights were 30 sarsen lintels,
   secured on the uprights and linked by tongue-and-groove joints, to make a
   continuous ring of stone more than 5 m (16 ft) up in the air.

2 Stonehenge from the air, at the time when visitors could walk freely among the stones. The central stone setting is only about 30 m (100 ft) across.
Photograph from the library of the Cambridge University Air Photograph Collection.

- an *inner circle* of much smaller upright stones, without lintels. These are igneous rocks, *bluestones*, whose geological origin is Wales.
- an *outer horseshoe* of ten upright sarsens set as five pairs each with a single lintel.
- an *inner horseshoe* of upright bluestones without lintels.
- a single stone of Welsh sandstone, now lying flat, at the apex of the horseshoe. In recent times it has been called the *Altar Stone*.

The whole makes a structure of symmetrical design, arranged around an axis that runs north-east to south-west, and facing north-east.

This main ruin is encircled by the worn remains of a circular bank-and-ditch, of about 100 m (330 ft) diameter. Just inside the earth bank are two *Station Stones*, survivors of an original four. On the north-east side there is a break in the bank-and-ditch, where an earthwork Avenue runs out from the site. Near the break in the bank is a fallen stone, the *Slaughter Stone*, and outside one still standing, the *Heel Stone*.

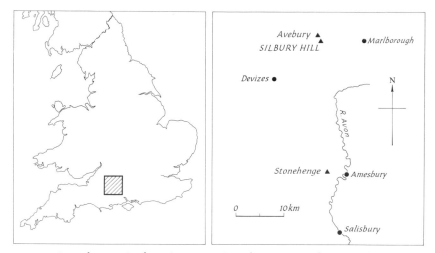

3 Stonehenge: its location near Amesbury in southern England.
Map by Arthur Shelley.

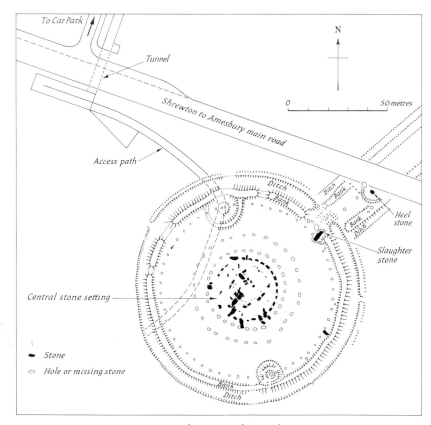

4 Major features of Stonehenge.
Plan by Arthur Shelley.

Archaeological study has revealed traces of other features, such as a circle of *Aubrey holes* just inside the bank, which are now invisible on the surface.

In the modern archaeological view, Stonehenge is not a single-period site, although the main ruin is a coherent structure erected about 2000 BC. But some elements, the bank-and-ditch and Heel Stone, for example, are 1000 or more years older, and others are several hundred years younger.

The landscape around Stonehenge contains a great many earthworks and traces of ancient human activity, of broadly the period of Stonehenge itself, many of them burial mounds and other places that suggest sacred ceremonial more than secular settlement − if, that is, sacred and secular divide neatly.

THE FORGETTING AND THE RE-DISCOVERY OF STONEHENGE

Once upon a time, Stonehenge was a new place. Then, New Stonehenge − or whatever it was called − became Old Stonehenge. Old Stonehenge was in time abandoned and forgotten, as happens in the end to every human creation, however magnificent in its own era. It figures in no classical author's mention of Britain, nor in the first medieval histories of England.

Since then a variety of individuals and groups, with a variety of individual and group interests, have taken an interest in Stonehenge. Here that variety is sketched in, as preparation for those particular claims that are set out later in the book.

The first sign of its re-discovery is not in a literary text, but in its very name, Stonehenge. Deriving from the Old English *stan* and *hencg* or *hen(c)gen*, it shows notice had been taken of it before its first manuscript mention by scholars of the new Norman-French learning. It was acclaimed, about the year 1130, as one of the wonders of England, and a full history of the building of Stonehenge was given in Geoffrey of Monmouth's *History of England* a few years later, on the misapprehension that it belonged to a period after the Roman occupation of Britain.

A first fair picture of Stonehenge dates to about 1573–5, when the Flemish artist and topographer Lucas de Heere drew a perspective of the stones 'as I myself have drawn them on the spot' . The next century saw much interest in the place. The diarists Samuel Pepys, John Evelyn and Celia Fiennes all paid visits, Evelyn noticing that the stones of the 'stupendious Monument' were 'so exceeding hard that all my strength with a hammer, could not breake a fragment'. So did King James I, who visited Stonehenge in 1620 and was so intrigued that he had his architect Inigo Jones study it for him. Jones's book, *Stone-heng Restored*, published by his nephew and colleague John Webb in 1655, is the first full-length study of any prehistoric antiquity.

5 This painting, by Richard Tongue (1837) shows how the surviving stones make an open horseshoe or 'cell', open towards the south-east.
By permission of the British Museum.

Stonehenge has been a central subject of study by antiquarians and archaeologists ever since (fig. 5). Many of the major individuals in British archaeology have made especial study of Stonehenge and its context, from John Aubrey and William Stukeley in the earliest days of antiquarian fieldwork, to Richard Colt Hoare and John Lubbock as archaeology was established as a systematic, scientific discipline, and to Stuart Piggott and Richard Atkinson in our own day.

THE LEGAL OWNERSHIP OF STONEHENGE AS A PHYSICAL OBJECT

The history of the ownership of Stonehenge is known over the last six centuries; it shows its gradual transfer from the private property of its landowner, to treat as he wished, into a public ownership.

In medieval times the land around Stonehenge belonged to the manor of

Amesbury, and was used for pasture and arable. Stonehenge itself is not mentioned in surviving records of the medieval period, but its ownership presumably went with the land on which it stood. In any case it had no economic value, and its stones were protected 'by their own Weight & Worthlessness', although it is recorded from the seventeenth century that blocks were taken away to make bridges.

During the seventeenth century, the ownership of the west Amesbury estate, and of Stonehenge, passed from a Robert Newdyk, to Sir Lawrence Washington of Garsdon (an ancestor of the first President of the United States), and then to a Thomas Hayward, who implanted a colony of rabbits and was granted, in 1680, a Royal Warrant to hold an annual fair at Stonehenge each September. In 1778 ownership passed with the estate to the fourth Marquess of Queensberry, who is not known to have taken an active interest, although he did refuse permission for antiquarians to restore to the upright a trilithon which fell in 1797.

On Queensberry's death, the Amesbury estate was bought by Sir Edmund Antrobus. Proud to call himself 'the proprietor of Stonehenge', Antrobus thought Stonehenge should be left in peace. He took his architect's advice about propping stones, and had his under-gamekeeper dig out the colony of rabbits. But he would not 'improve' it, allow archaeologists to excavate the place, or let General Pitt-Rivers, the first Inspector of Ancient Monuments, tell him how to care for it. A series of guardians looked after Stonehenge during the nineteenth century by arrangement with Antrobus: the guardians sold water-colours, models and, later, photographs to the visitors, and took their tips in exchange for trying to keep Stonehenge safe from the camp-fires, rubbish and litter of visitors and their horses, and from the hammers of souvenir-hunters.

The previous century, Stonehenge had already been so busy that an enterprising Amesbury carpenter made a living selling liquor and refreshments from a smoky hut dug against a stone, and Stukeley complained of the 'infinite number of daily visitants'. By the late nineteenth century Stonehenge was so popular that *The Times* thought it 'in danger of being vulgarized out of all knowledge and certainly out of all its venerable charms. To continue to allow this marvellous relic of prehistoric ages to be ruthlessly disfigured and perish inch by inch would be an eternal disgrace.'

In 1898, Edmund Antrobus died, and was succeeded by his nephew. The new Baronet felt Stonehenge was a dubious asset to the estate, yielding no income yet a source of trouble. So he offered to sell it with its downland to the Government for £125,000, a price valuing the historical associations of the place so high that the Chancellor of the Exchequer thought it 'absolutely impossible for any purchaser to consider'. Rumours were put about that 'the owner might be tempted by some American millionaire who may be inclined to bid for notoriety by transporting the relic bodily across the Atlantic'; but it was also observed, 'one only has to threaten the Government with a rich American, and the price might be raised indefinitely'. No American purchaser materialized, nor did a showman who would take on Stonehenge as a commercial undertaking, nor an advertising business wanting a 'Pear's Soap Stone'.

All this time, Stonehenge had stood unfenced and free on the open downs, with tracks running through between the stones. After the fall of two stones in 1900, Antrobus fenced Stonehenge in, diverting the tracks, and charging a shilling's admission to visitors (there were 3770 the first year); a High Court case, in 1905, supported his right to do so, against the claim 'for the free use by the public of Stonehenge as a place of resort'.

The Amesbury estate was broken up and sold by auction in September 1915. Lot 15, Stonehenge and a little triangle of land round it, made £6,600. The purchaser was a local landowner, Mr Cecil Chubb of Bemerton. In 1918, Chubb gave Stonehenge to the Government, and was rewarded with a knighthood. Since then, Stonehenge has been managed by the government department concerned with ancient monuments, first by the Office of Works, then by the Ministry of Works, then by the Ministry of Public Building and Works, then by the Department of the Environment, and since 1983, by English Heritage, the quasi-independent agency which government has made responsible for looking after the ancient sites of England.

The Chubb gift secured Stonehenge from chance sale, export or exploitation. But during and after the First World War its environs had become cluttered and shabby, with a Stonehenge Aerodrome on the west (after the war, converted into a store for surplus government bricks and then into a Stonehenge pig-farm), a Stonehenge café, new cottages for Stonehenge custodians, and talk of a Stonehenge bungalow colony. A public appeal 'to restore and preserve the open surroundings' of Stonehenge raised, in 1927–9, the funds to buy 600 ha (1500 acres) around the monument. The land was vested in the National Trust as 'inalienable', to keep it safe in perpetuity, and the clutter of buildings was erased.

The land ownership is much the same now. English Heritage manages Stonehenge and the little patch of land round it, with archaeological and tourist interests in mind. The National Trust manages most of the environs, which are farmed commercially but with a primary regard also for appearance, amenity, and archaeological conservation. The two roads which run close by Stonehenge, the A344 Amesbury to Devizes highway to the north, and the A303 London to Exeter trunk road to the south, are the responsibility of Wiltshire County Council and the Department of Transport. Public utility services, such as the 'Stonehenge cable', a telephone line whose trench was cut through precious archaeological deposits 20 years ago, run along the road verges. The land further away on three sides is owned by farmers, who are under some legal constraints to ensure proper care for identified ancient monuments on their holdings. On the last, the northern side, is part of the Army's Salisbury Plain Training Area, owned by the Ministry of Defence.

STONEHENGE AND ARCHAEOLOGICAL
UNDERSTANDING

Stonehenge has been a subject and inspiration for artists over many centuries, especially in the heyday of English landscape water-colourists; Turner's and Constable's pictures of Stonehenge are considered among their masterpieces. That tradition continues: there are fine prints of Stonehenge by Henry Moore, and an exhibition of Stonehenge pictures in 1987 found no shortage of brand-new images of the place, by painters, photographers, and print-makers.

But these inspirational visions of Stonehenge are conventionally regarded as secondary. Stonehenge is recognized to be a prehistoric monument, removed by 4000 or so years from our own direct knowledge of the world and by 2000 or so from the earliest historical references to Britain. It is a prehistoric thing, and expert knowledge of Stonehenge is due to the archaeologists, as the scientists reckoned to be expert in these matters. Heterodox views exist, some of them very odd indeed, but the understanding of archaeologists in matters concerning archaeology has not much been challenged. It is their business to know about these things.

What is their understanding of Stonehenge, and how is it arrived at?

Archaeologists, and before them antiquarians of a less consciously 'scientific' bent, have been exploring Stonehenge and its environs for over three centuries, surveying what is visible on the surface, digging for what is underneath, and studying what they find there. Excavation at Stonehenge itself began in the 1620s, when a hole 'about the bignesse of two sawe pitts' was dug by the Duke of Buckingham. Much more than half the area of Stonehenge has been excavated at one time or another, with varying results. No riches or treasure have been found, at least in recent times, and the archaeological finds from Stonehenge make a large and very drab collection; for the most part, it consists of chips and dust from the great stones, broken pieces of flint and chalk, and the miscellaneous debris and rubbish left by visitors over the centuries. But it is this evidence, amplified in recent years by physical-science techniques and by the study of broadly comparable sites of a similar period, that provides the archaeological account.

Stonehenge is not a single structure or a single site; rather, the material above and below ground derives from a series of earth, timber and stone structures, revised and re-modelled over a period of more than 2000 years, from about 3200 BC to perhaps 1100 BC. The great structure of trilithons belongs to about the middle of this period. A very great deal of detailed information exists about the specifics of the site, concerning not just its human artefacts but also its environment; for example, the mollusc shells from successive buried soils give a detailed account of the kinds of snails that have lived at Stonehenge, thence of vegetation at the site, since snails are finicky about these things, and thence an indication as to when people kept the place clear of scrub and when they let bushes grow.

Archaeologists are concerned with prehistoric people as well as prehistoric objects, and there is a social interpretation to go with the physical and environmental evidence. Stonehenge is seen as a central place, the social and ritual focus for the communities who lived in its region, one of four or five distinct territories of Neolithic Wessex; other ceremonial and burial monuments in the environs of Stonehenge make the whole area a ritual landscape. The structural complexities of the Stonehenge phases span a period covering a transition from an egalitarian society, based on lineages and respectful of family ancestors, to a 'chiefdom' society, with a distinct class of chiefs wielding individual power. The shifting form of Stonehenge is seen as reflecting these changing social and ritual emphases in Neolithic and Bronze Age communities.

Nothing whatever in history or in prehistory can be a matter of absolute and certain proof. There is no possibility of going back to see prehistoric Stonehenge directly. An archaeologist or other researcher can examine only what is available now, in the modern world, and make such deductions as he can from those modern observations of what has survived from the past.

That said, the physical evidence from Stonehenge seems fairly secure, despite an unhappy history of study and publication. There are uncertainties in the sequence and in the phasing, but of a technical nature. The overall pattern, of a series of structures over a long period centred about 2000 BC, has not changed very much, though there is still much to revise and refine in the detail.

Like all archaeological knowledge, the archaeological understanding of Stonehenge is of a certain character, and three things need to be said about it.

Firstly, it is – and should be – knowledge of a secular and sceptical nature, if it is to be a scientific knowledge. It should be founded on testable propositions and uniformitarian principles, and it should not be directed by matters of faith or emotion. Archaeology works, necessarily, by comparative methods: a place like Stonehenge is so unusual that, in applying comparative methods, one risks comparing it with things not really comparable.

Secondly, the archaeological knowledge of Stonehenge becomes more precarious as it moves from physical evidence to social and religious inference. The account made from the snail shells rests on the ecological preferences of the same species of creatures today. But the proposal that the later structures at Stonehenge are the work of a 'chiefdom society' rests upon less certain analogies with recent societies in, principally, Polynesia, on generalizations about the nature of chiefdom societies, and on ideas about what kinds of monuments chiefdom societies build. Behind phrases like 'social and ritual centre', 'central place' or 'ritual landscape' are uncertain and vague concepts. Much depends on which analogies are chosen, which generalizations are preferred, even on which of several words is used to describe an observation: the alignment of the

Stonehenge axis approximately towards the direction of midsummer sunrise can be called 'ritual', 'religious', 'astronomical', or 'calendrical' – different words which describe differences, not of physical evidence, but in the view people living in the modern world choose to take of that evidence.

There is nothing wrong with that use of analogy and generalization, or with inferring from the physical evidence as we can observe it today to the prehistoric people we cannot see. Without them, nothing can be said about the people of prehistory, at Stonehenge or anywhere else. And the same must and does apply to non-archaeologists who choose, like archaeologists, to study the past by the evidence we have in the present.

There is another consequence. When archaeologists move on, to a more imaginative evocation from their special area of competence in dealing with those things that can reliably be deduced from specific kinds of physical evidence, they are moving out into areas where what seems like a good foundation of empirical knowledge, and of techniques to work with that empirical knowledge, is of less relevance. It is not clear to me that an archaeologist has any special expertise when he says of Stonehenge:

> It is a dark place, oppressive as though Death were lurking in its shadows. The sarsens are thick, crowding against each other, forced deep into the ground by the lintels heavily pressing down upon them. It is a jostle of stone, monumental but overbearing, and the gaps between the pillars are no more than slits of light through the dark stonework of the circle. Inside the barrier of the sarsens the trilithons climb tightly together, shadowing the sky, grim, sombre, elegiac as though mourning the twilight of mortality.[1]

Dr Aubrey Burl, author of these words and an acknowledged expert on stone rings, may feel all this, but in the absence of relevant comparative analogue, he has no reliable grounds for proposing that prehistoric people inside Stonehenge felt the place to be either deathly oppressive (as he chooses to think) or comfortably protective (as it was for Tess of the d'Urbervilles, when she sheltered inside Stonehenge in Thomas Hardy's novel; and as it is for me). In this evocation, the archaeologist has no especial expertise. It may even confuse the issue, if he mixes up his amateur thoughts on this matter with his expertise in matters archaeological.

These, then, make up the variety of aspects which are the archaeological view of Stonehenge: a considerable and tolerably secure body of descriptive evidence derived from the physical – a body of evidence which seems to have grown more secure; a superstructure of reasoned inference from that evidence which depends also on comparative study – a more transient superstructure which has changed over decades and centuries in some obedience to things other than the physical evidence; and a penumbra of individual evocations not wholly different in character from those of artists, poets, visionaries, and cranks.

the liquids, and the smoother Altar Stone at the centre, where the cleaned and burnt sacrifice was offered. There is absolutely no evidence that either interpretation is justified, the popularity of the names still perhaps indicating more about our visions of our great ancient monuments than about the monument itself.

STONEHENGE AS A CELTIC SYMBOL, AND THE STONEHENGE DRUIDS

All over Wales are stone circles, not just ancient monuments but modern Gorsedd circles put up at *eisteddfodau*, the bardic celebrations which have become central to the nurture of Welsh culture and the Welsh language. The Gorsedd circles are one of many strands that can be traced back to the linking of ancient stone circles to the Druids, and with that linking to the conscious re-making and revival of things Druidical. Another strand, quite different in character, is the prominent place of Druids and stone circles in the visionary works of William Blake.

Once Stonehenge was accepted as a work of the Britons, it was logical to link it to the Celts, as the known ethnic affiliation of the Britons in earliest historical times – the Britons who survived in the highlands of western and northern Britain beyond the common reach of the series of invaders, Roman, Anglo-Saxon, Viking, Norman. So stone circles, as symbols and relics of that British and Celtic culture, were taken up by the Celtic, and especially the Welsh, cultural revival of the nineteenth century as emblems of the Celtic spirit (hence the building of Gorsedd circles, though in fact there is no evidence of association between the prehistoric Celts and stone circles, the latter being much earlier). Archaeologists of the nineteenth century commonly called the stone circles and chamber tombs 'Celtic antiquities', as opposed to the 'antediluvial' flint implements from glacial gravels.

As Stukeley had formed a Society of Roman Knights, so an Ancient Order of Druids was formed late in the eighteenth century; it seems to have been a secret society, rather on the model of freemasonry. Since then there have been a variety of Druidical orders, some primarily social, some reviving Druidism as a religious belief. It was only in the early years of this century, that members of Druid orders started going to Stonehenge to worship, most often at the midsummer solstice.

Twentieth-century archaeologists, noting the span of time that separates modern Druids from ancient Druids, the span of time that separates ancient Druids from the building of Stonehenge, and the Romantic enthusiasms that surrounded the Celtic revival, have for the most part regarded the modern Druid orders, and their Stonehenge celebrations, as bogus, the rump end of an antique historical error which should have expired when the chronological place of Stonehenge in prehistory was understood.

STONEHENGE AS A SECULAR PLACE

Whether or not they represent an historical continuity with ancient Druids, and whether or not any continuity with ancient Druids is with people who had anything to do with Stonehenge, the modern Druid orders maintain an attitude to Stonehenge which at least echoes the prehistoric one. Stonehenge, in almost every opinion, was a place of religion and ritual in prehistory. The modern Druids treat it that way today; the State as custodians of the place, and archaeologists as scientists, do not.

It is disconcerting to see how much the character of a sacred place changes when it becomes secular. The process is sadly visible today in English cathedrals, now that most of their visitors no longer have religious beliefs; they do not know the logic and liturgy of Christian faith which determines, or used to determine, what the building is for and how it works. In those cathedrals, like Ely, which are assertive in managing themselves as business-like tourist centres, the religious uses of the building seem to have become secondary. A 'voluntary' donation is asked for most firmly at the door. The café has been spruced up. The souvenir shop has crept over more of the south aisle. The clerestorey is now a museum, with an extra admission fee. The cathedral was, until bought off by a philanthropist, planning to build new houses in its precincts. While the main cathedral is occupied with the annual flower festival, Christian worshippers are admitted, free of charge, into one of the small side-chapels, as if worship was no longer the real point of the place but a marginal use to be tolerated. All this is arranged to make the income to keep the building up. No wonder that some radical Christians feel that religion is in the heart, not the building, and think the Church should abandon these places as a material burden to real religious practice.

If the secular atmosphere of Ely reflects the remoteness of today's tourists, a generation away from those who shared a faith with those who built the place, how much further removed are visitors to Stonehenge, 4000 years older and how many religious reformations more distant?

For almost every visitor, Stonehenge is a secular place, at least when it comes to the specifics of religious belief – perhaps necessarily, unless one thinks that the Druid orders have re-discovered, or never lost, the authentic faith that inspired Stonehenge. The archaeological attitude to Stonehenge, while recognizing Stonehenge as a place of ritual, is wholly secular; archaeologists aim towards a scientific understanding, some kind of disinterested sociology of prehistoric religion, rather than a re-affirmation or re-creation of a prehistoric faith.

THE CHALLENGE OF STONEHENGE ASTRONOMY

The strongest recent challenge to archaeological authority over Stonehenge has come from the revival of ideas that its design was largely structured by

7 Close-up of the lichens that cloak the stones.
Photograph by Christopher Chippindale.

astronomical alignments. Stukeley, two and a half centuries before, had noticed that the axis of symmetry of Stonehenge, and the earthwork avenue that led from it, were directed towards the north-east, 'where abouts the sun rises when the days are longest'. A series of researchers, most famously the astronomer Sir Norman Lockyer at the turn of this century, have elaborated the idea. In 1963 C. A. Newham discovered other astronomical alignments, to solar and to lunar events. Then the astronomer Gerald Hawkins of Boston University published two papers in *Nature* and a hugely successful book, *Stonehenge Decoded*[3], that set out the case that Stonehenge was a 'neolithic observatory-cum-computer', where precise observations could be combined with arithmetic computations made with moving stones accurately to forecast eclipses. An intermittent argument has wrangled on since over the reality of Stonehenge astronomy, in Newham's, Hawkins's, and other variants. There were notable early contributions from Professor Fred Hoyle, who was much impressed by the skills of prehistoric Stonehenge astronomers – 'A veritable Newton or Einstein must have been at work.' And Professor Alexander Thom, who had been working on the astronomy, geometry and mensuration of stone circles for some years, in time came to Stonehenge and elaborated another astronomical view of its role.

There followed some years of confusion, whilst the astronomical propositions were examined, in their own terms and by reference to archaeological considerations. Archaeologists found much to criticize, for example, in the incorporating together into astronomical schemas of different elements in and around Stonehenge that could be dated with a good confidence to periods many centuries apart.

Opinion about the nature and even the existence of Stonehenge astronomy remains divided – in part because very few people have a sufficient understanding of archaeology and of astronomy to be able to work comfortably with both approaches.

The common opinion among prehistoric archaeologists is that there are alignments and orientations at Stonehenge and other ancient sites that relate to solar and lunar events, but not a great many, and made with no very great

8 The remarkable winter sunset, here used on the cover of a book catalogue.

precision. These are not systems that can be called 'astronomy', with its overtones of white-coated scientists using exact mathematics. Stonehenge is not an 'observatory', still less a 'computer'. The regularities are better thought of as *calendrical*, relating to the seasonal patterns, and to a ritual or religious concern for those patterns which is understandable enough in the context of a farming society. A cathedral like Ely is aligned towards an astronomical event, the rising of the sun, for a religious reason which is not sun worship, but it is not an observatory and its priests are not astronomers; the same may go for Stonehenge.

Many astronomers seem convinced by the case for Stonehenge astronomy. Stonehenge commonly features now in general astronomy books, as a first relic of systematic astronomy, and Stonehenge has figured prominently in public-relations films for NASA: as men once reached for the stars with Stonehenge, reaching to the limits of contemporary technology in a great adventure of science, so do we today with the space programme.

The public who come to see Stonehenge commonly favour the astronomical view. Certainly this is the impression I have gained in talking to visitors over the years, and the publicity that envelops Stonehenge each midsummer sunrise encourages the idea. And the image of Stonehenge against the rising sun has become one of the most famous and recognizable of archaeological pictures.

Stonehenge astronomy is the major intellectual challenge to archaeological authority. The archaeologists have, for the moment, lost that tussle; unluckily, in my view, as I think the astronomical theories of Stonehenge as a prehistoric observatory, computer or eclipse-predicting engine are not supported by enough good evidence. But this is a separate issue, to do with differences of opinion between groups of scientists with different interests and different backgrounds, largely separate from the questions which this book explores.[4]

SOFT PRIMITIVES AND HARD PRIMITIVES AT STONEHENGE

The lining-up of a pair of stones in the design of Stonehenge on the direction of, say, the midwinter sunrise can be seen as no ordering of any kind – since any two stones necessarily make a line in some direction or other, and the horizon is full of calendrically and astronomically significant directions where sun, moon, stars and planets have risen or set. A main reason for the absence of a decisive resolution of the question of Stonehenge astronomy is that a number of these alignments would arise by chance, as they do in modern buildings planned without any astronomical or calendrical concerns; the point is not that there *are* alignments, but in whether they are so *many* or of *such a nature* that they are probably not due to chance.

If alignments are regarded as significant, they can be seen either as calendric ordering within a temple, or as astronomical ordering within an observatory. The physical evidence is the same – a set of stones, holes and other features in a certain observed spatial order. The source of difference is not in the evidence, but in the attitudes with which the evidence is approached.

Differences of this kind go back to the beginning of Stonehenge studies. In the seventeenth century, Inigo Jones emphasized the graces of Stonehenge. Since the Britons, 'a savage and barbarous People, knowing no use at all of garments', could not have constructed a building 'of as beautiful *Proportions*, as elegant in *Order*, and as Stately in *Aspect*, as any', Jones concluded Stonehenge was Roman. His friend and opponent Edmund Bolton saw different qualities in the same shapes, those 'orderly irregular, and formlesse uniforme heaps of massive marble' – 'that STONAGE was a worke of the Britanns, the rudenesse it selfe perswades'.

Behind these views of Stonehenge are two fundamentally opposed views of the distant past that run through historical opinions of every age. A 'soft primitive' view thinks people might have been 'gentle, loving and faithful, void of all guile and treason, and living after the manner of the Golden Age' – in the words of an early European traveller to the Americas. A 'hard primitive' view was famously put by Thomas Hobbes in his *Leviathan* of 1651, of people 'in continuall feare, and danger of violent death; And the life of man, solitary, poore, nasty, brutish and shorte'.

The ancient Druids of Stonehenge have been hard and soft also, and so have seemed the modern Druids: in the 1920s the Chief Druid MacGregor Reid found it necessary to lay public and ritual curses on custodians and other enemies at Stonehenge, and to announce their fatal efficacy, while the Druids today make no threats.

There may be a tendency for archaeologists to favour hard primitive views: partly because archaeological data derives for the most part from the broken scraps and ruins of a technology that is, by the twentieth century's view of the world, brutishly backward; partly because there seems unequivocal evidence of short life-spans and great toil; partly because the qualities and values that we see as making human lives happy in nasty material circumstances seem not of a nature to leave direct physical traces. Since Stonehenge seems unusually, even uniquely, accomplished among monuments of the period, in its refinement and engineering, the overall vision archaeologists have is of a period more backward in those aspects.

By comparison Stonehenge astronomy and the wider 'megalithic science', putting together skills of geometry, mensuration and astronomy, offered a softer and a nobler vision – or so it seemed (for an astronomer, like any other human being, can also be a cruel beast, and a motive offered for the interest in astronomy was the value of eclipse-production for an élite anxious to keep its standing and power).

The empirical evidence from prehistoric Stonehenge is ambivalent, of course – that is why hardily and softly primitive Stonehenges have stood alongside each other for centuries. In a conventional western grouping of traits, the skills of Stonehenge can seem the soft and learned ones of deft craftsmanship, geometric precision, a nice aesthetic appreciation, and an overall achievement that indicates the cooperative and collaborative work of a whole community. And even if the general pattern of prehistoric British life looks to be hardily primitive – with its scrappy huts, clumsy pottery and rude mechanicals of megalithic buildings with rough, unshaped slabs – the features of engineering excellence that are special to Stonehenge may tell a different, softer story.

A noticeable feature of the tenor of British prehistory in the 1980s has been a softening of archaeologists' primitives. Empirical evidence, for the ordered management of coppice woodland or the large-scale division of land at very much earlier periods than used to be known, has helped make the builders of Stonehenge seem a little more advanced, a little more like us. And the mood has perceptibly changed too. A major exhibition in 1985, 'Symbols of Power at the time of Stonehenge', advertised itself with nakedness as beautiful rather than rude, and distributed badges with the slogan, 'I'm no squat, grunting savage.'

STONEHENGE AND EARTH MYSTERIES

At much the same time as the astronomers disputed the archaeologists' dismal view of the scientific skills of the people of Stonehenge, there was a perceptible strengthening of another opinion, that catholic body of researchers outside the archaeological mainstream that is represented in this book by Paul Devereux. He calls this manner of work 'earth mystery studies', and in his presence I make no amateur attempt to summarize it here.

Earth mystery researchers think that archaeologists have gone largely wrong, both in the aspects of ancient things they choose to study and in how they envisage prehistoric ways of life and world-views. Archaeologists do not recognize important classes of earth-mystery evidence, like the long-distance alignments or 'leys' which they see as the haphazard consequences of chance in landscapes well-scattered with ancient sites; and they feel that dowsing or mapping fields of force around ancient places is going too far towards the woolly delusions of the para-normal.

Stonehenge astronomers made, fundamentally, much the same charge, and there is an overlap between the two groups both in evidence, especially of alignments between stones and between sites, and in attitude. John Michell, *doyen* of earth mystery studies, sets out that coincidence and his own philosophical frame of thinking about the past, in introducing his *Little History of Astro-archaeology*, subtitled *Stages in the Transformation of a Heresy*:

In these pages we follow the rise of an archaeological theory which relates the designs and locations of megalithic sites to the observed positions of the heavenly bodies at the time they were constructed. The idea seems harmless enough, but it arouses passions; for behind the question of whether or not the megalith builders four thousand years ago practised scientific astronomy there are other, more serious issues; and these concern the history and very nature of civilization. Two historical world views are here displayed in mutual opposition. The modern view, informed by the theory of evolutionary progress, is of civilization as a recent and unique phenomenon. Against this is the older orthodoxy of Plato and the pagan philosophers, that civilization proceeds in cycles, from primitive settlement, through the development of agriculture and technology, to empire, decadence and oblivion – a pattern of events constantly repeated. The first of these beliefs, enshrined in modern orthodoxy, serves to justify many of the political and academic modes now dominant. It will not therefore lightly give way before its rival.[5]

THE STONEHENGE FESTIVAL

If earth mystery studies are the theory for one different view of Stonehenge and of what Stonehenge was about, then the Druids and the festival are the practice and the action.

The Druids, mentioned above, have numbered a few score at the Stonehenge solstice; their manner has been very gentle, and they may, as was recognized in 1987, continue there under official tolerance. It is sometimes said that Druids have worshipped at Stonehenge for a century or more; this may be so, but the first documentary record of a Druid meeting at Stonehenge is of a mass induction into the Ancient Order in August 1905 – not at the summer solstice. (It was, by the newspaper accounts, not entirely a sober affair. The mass induction of several hundred blindfolded novices was preceded by a grand lunch in a marquee just by Stonehenge, at which a famous quantity of drink was downed.) Solstice ceremonies came a few years after.

The Stonehenge festival has been a larger gathering, 35,000 strong in some estimates, until it was suppressed in 1984. It began in 1974 when, a reliable source explains:

Phil Russel, commonly known as Wally Hope, established the Stonehenge People's Free Festival. His followers, all of whom claimed the name Wally and were collectively called The Wallies, camped in fields near the site which they declared sacred ground. Their festival and those which followed were of a pagan religious character. Babies were baptized and marriages were performed at the stones on the longest day. Wally Hope was arrested and sent to prison, and soon afterwards he died in unexplained circumstances. At the Wallies' second festival, in 1975, his ashes were ceremonially scattered among the stones.

Syd Rawles, later an acknowledged leader of the festival community, explained in 1978 why the festival was at Stonehenge specifically:

We come to Stonehenge because in an unstable world it is proper that the people should look to the past in order to learn for the future. . . . Stonehenge and the surrounding area is one of the most powerful spiritual centres in Europe. It is right that we should meekly stand in the presence of God, but it is proper that we should now sing and dance and shout for joy.

Over some years, the festival established a routine of running for a few weeks before the solstice in the field across the road north-west of Stonehenge. An important element for some people was its religious character; and for a scattered travelling community on the social margin, the festival was an important symbol, the main occasion for that community to meet together. The festival's fly-posted publicity put the emphasis on 'sex and drugs and rock'n'roll' (all this was, remember, in the era before AIDS).

The festival never had the blessing of the National Trust, on whose land it squatted unlawfully, and no proper facilities for sanitation or rubbish disposal were arranged. Stonehenge itself was defended each year by barbed-wire entanglements, and farmers blocked field entrances round about. In law the festival's trespass was a civil rather than a criminal matter, so the police kept only a watching brief; in later years, when commercial drug-dealing was more conspicuous, and violent incidents were reported, they were more active.

The 'official' attitude towards the festival – as an unpleasant nuisance that would have to be tolerated until it fizzled out – changed for 1985, when the National Trust and English Heritage announced a ban on the festival, and on the Druids as well, since Stonehenge would be closed over the solstice to prevent intrusion. That year the police, on their own initiative, took a most active interest, and stopped the festival convoy at Cholderton, on the road to Stonehenge. An often-violent 'Battle of Stonehenge' ensued in a bean field, between police and convoy. There were 520 arrests and many accusations of police misbehaviour. The prosecutions of convoy members were mostly lost when they came to court, long after the solstice had passed without a festival or Druid presence. An enquiry was critical of the police action and the behaviour of individual officers. In 1986 and 1987, the festival convoy was again stopped a distance from Stonehenge. In 1988 Druid ceremonies took place on the road near Stonehenge, rather than at the site itself, hemmed by lines of police and with police helicopters circling overhead. In 1989 Stonehenge was again officially defended against convoy, Druids and festival.

The festival affair, and the suppression of the convoy, was partly about Stonehenge, partly about wider social issues, as we explore later.

STONEHENGE TODAY

'Everyone can go to the seaside, but if everyone does, then no one will have the beach to themselves.'

The ideal experience of Stonehenge, as agreed over the centuries, is to wander alone among its stones. But everyone, or at least several hundreds of thousand of people, go to see it each year, and it is much smaller than the average beach.

The history of managing Stonehenge is a dismal one, of a losing battle against the success of the place. Victorians found its atmosphere already gone:

> Waggonette parties are the bane of Stonehenge. To avoid them you must be up with the dawn, or you must wait for the evening shadows. Unfortunately I had stumbled upon the early afternoon, and long before I had reached the stones I could see that they were ringed with a cordon of waggonettes and flecked with the light foam of summer blouses.[6]

Despite the guardians, picnics and horses left their litter behind (unpleasant though the oily droppings of modern cars may be, horses used to leave larger traces). Souvenir-hunters bashed away at the stones (when Charles Darwin visited Stonehenge, the guardian was grateful he had not brought a hammer but was amenable to any amount of digging).

That ceased, largely, with the fencing of Stonehenge in 1901, and an attempt to return Stonehenge to rural peace. Since then Stonehenge has been overwhelmed. A busy road runs through the north edge of the site, and the main London to Exeter highway a couple of hundred metres to the south. Inescapable demands for visitor facilities – car- and coach-parking, lavatories, a souvenir shop, a café – have been met by a squalid little development, just across the road from Stonehenge. It is on the land that was purchased by national subscription and vested for its safety in the care of the National Trust expressly to prevent its piecemeal conversion into cafés and so on. A grass, and then a gravel, surface among the stones could not stand the press of feet, and now visitors cannot normally go into Stonehenge; instead they walk on a tarmac path from which it is very hard properly to appreciate what is there. We have reached the position where so many people try to see Stonehenge that very few see it properly.

Gina Maranto, writing in the American magazine *Discover* in 1985, describes the experience of visiting Stonehenge in the official manner today:

> Let's get it straight. Stonehenge 1985 is no place of mystery. It's not intriguing, evocative, or powerful enough to drive away thoughts of the twentieth century and leave you there, at the hub of Salisbury Plain, awestruck as you look out over the landscape of prehistory.

No, on a sunny summer day when a mob of tourists descends on it, visiting England's best known example of neolithic architecture is about as inspiring as shopping at Bloomingdale's on Christmas Eve. You drive around the parking lot, and then the overflow parking lot, for ten, fifteen minutes, waiting for a slot; navigate through the loitering crowds of sightseers licking their prepackaged Walls Ice Cream cones; pay your £1 entrance fee; trudge through the concrete tunnel under A344 [the main road], come up wham-bam on the north side of Stonehenge, and make a disappointing circuit fifty yards from the stones, peering to make out details and trying hard to ignore the reedy voice of some fubsy matron from Boca Raton declaiming at the top of her lungs, 'But it's so dinky, Harold. Why is it so dinky?'[7]

Maranto's account is reasonable, though it does not attempt to be kind. The Stonehenge she experienced had nothing to it of that rich and optimistic view of Stonehenge which underlies so many visions of the place today – whether the Druids and elements of the festival, with their regard for Stonehenge as a place of real and continued religious meaning; whether the astronomers, with their finding it a place of advanced learning and science; or, come to that, the archaeologists who find it the most remarkable building achievement of

9 A dismal design of the late 1960s sets the official facilities at Stonehenge in a grey concrete box, half underground.
Photograph by Christopher Chippindale.

prehistoric Europe. Instead, there is a cheap mess, a lack of respect for the place (fig. 9); and worse, in the summer months of recent years when the expectant world and his wife come in their daily thousands, the site is festooned in barbed-wire, surrounded by police, and patrolled by privately-employed security guards with dogs. It has looked like a concentration camp, the unacceptable face of militarism in a democracy. The reality of the festival has been physically filthy and expensive too, as the National Trust and its tenants found each year when it came to the July clean-up of the festival field. While it is easy enough to blame the shambles on the thousands of 'travellers', the national disgrace that is Stonehenge in the 1980s also asks questions of officialdom.

STONEHENGE TOMORROW

Nobody set out to make Stonehenge a cheap mess; it was simply that piecemeal provision and accommodation, without enough long-term planning, have added up to a cheap mess. So many agencies and interests are involved with Stonehenge and its environs that is is unfair to blame any one or to expect any one to be able radically to remedy things. In 1983 I glumly entitled a paper about why the mess had arisen 'What future for Stonehenge?'[8] because I did not expect to see anything much better.

After writing that, I was surprised at how general was the feeling that Stonehenge, with or without the festival, was in a disgraceful state. English Heritage on the day of its creation in 1984, announced a radical review of the presenting of Stonehenge. Five years later, very little has actually changed; perhaps I was right to be glum. Negotiations have dragged on with the military over a good plan to close the nearest main road and remove visitor facilities north a good distance to a new site at Larkhill. The diagnosis was right: the road is too intrusive, the facilities are too close, too small and too intrusive. The planned solution is right: to make open space around Stonehenge, to provide facilities at a better distance, and to let visitors approach Stonehenge on foot, as prehistoric people must have done.

Eventually, English Heritage got its scheme through — or thought it had, announcing in December 1989 that its Larkhill plan would go ahead. A new road would be built to provide car access. Local opinion was not happy, and a 'Save Stonehenge' (save Stonehenge from English Heritage, that is) campaign was immediately launched. At much the same time, English Heritage announced the Druids would be banned from Stonehenge for the 1990 midsummer solstice, guaranteeing there would be more trouble over the next year.

If the English Heritage plan ever becomes a reality, there will follow some nice decisions as to what interpretations of Stonehenge the new facilities will present and in what style. Will it be archaeology of an artefactual kind? Or archaeology as social theory, in the current intellectual fashion within the subject? Will the astronomy of Stonehenge be presented more as truth, after astronomical opinion, or more as misunderstanding, after archaeological opinion, or not at all, so as to offend neither party? Will the story of Stonehenge be a squeaky-clean tale of professional progress and archaeological knowledge, devoid of errors, mistakes and dissent? Will there be a place for Druids and dowsers in the Stonehenge of tomorrow? Will there be a resident artist or a visiting bard? Will the grass be managed by sheep or gangs of motor-mowers? And will there be a Foamhenge in the car-park for the kids to climb on?

Meanwhile we have the cheap mess. It is not of the archaeologists' making, but the archaeologists are the expert professionals on the official side of the Stonehenge divide. This archaeologist for one is embarrassed by the Stonehenge that visiting colleagues experience, and by the vision of the prehistoric past that it accidentally conveys.

We return to a tomorrow for Stonehenge at the end of the book.

CHAPTER TWO

STONEHENGE
AS AN EARTH
MYSTERY

Paul Devereux

The word 'geomancy' means, literally, 'earth divination'. It originally related to a form of fortune-telling using patterns created by the casting of a handful of earth. The Victorian missionaries, however, used the term to describe strange practices they encountered in places such as China,[1] where large, landscape-scale systems were carried out in which buildings had to have certain orientations, and sites and people had to be related to topographical features and strange energies (*ch'i* in the Chinese system) of the land and sky (fig. 10). The missionaries considered such behaviour to be superstitious, but acknowledged that these practices were based on a complex and coherent body of procedures. So the word 'geomancy' has been used in the sense of *sacred geography* for well over a hundred years, and is thus more established in the English language than certain other terms we use today.

By this perspective, Stonehenge is a geomantic centre. It stands as a symbol of the achievements of prehistoric peoples and, if geomancy is based on a detailed knowledge of the interaction between living systems and the planet, it is also a symbol of a forgotten science. The idea of certain places having intrinsic qualities has only become alien to the thought-patterns of Western culture since about the seventeenth century. But there is definite evidence that certain leaders even as late as Hitler believed that the occupation of geomantically important places would psychically consolidate martial conquest.[2] Stonehenge is thus a symbol, a multi-dimensional focus, of the landscape in which it is located – the physical, spiritual and social landscape of Britain (and is thus, to an extent, a symbol for Western consciousness as a whole). Many people see the recent controversy surrounding the midsummer usage of the site as symptomatic of the divisions within current British society, and of the clash of interests as to what is best for the country in social, political and economic terms. It has become a crisis of time and place on a number of levels. From this perspective it is only to be expected that one of the nation's key geomantic sites should come to general awareness at such a time.

10 The *feng shui* geomant at work in the Ch'ing dynasty.

Stonehenge is a symbol in another sense too. It provides cautioning fingers of stone pointing out of the mists of human history and experience that our modern form of knowledge may be so specialized that it has become fragmentary, that the *whole* is being lost in the parts. Archaeological discipline is fine, it is important, and we owe much of our appreciation of the past to it. (It is not, however, infallible, as Stonehenge reminds us; archaeology once thought that the Aubrey Holes were post-holes, a misconception now disproved, and until relatively recently the monument was thought to have been constructed with Mycenaean influence until a recalibration of carbon-dating corrected such a notion.) But ancient sites like Stonehenge can be approached in a variety of ways, using the perspectives granted by archaeology, archaeo-astronomy, folklore, geomancy, geometry, metrology, geology, geophysics and direct human experiential awareness.

EARTH MYSTERIES

This holistic, multi-disciplinary approach to the study of ancient sites is termed 'Earth Mysteries', for want of a better portmanteau term, by alternative researchers in Britain. It is their feeling that any approach to the understanding of ancient sacred places taken in exclusion to the others will inevitably lead to a distorted view. Moreover, Earth Mysteries researchers do not study ancient monuments as a form of genteel antiquarianism, but to see if fundamental principles regarding harmony between mind, body, spirit and planet can be learned from ancient peoples; principles which can perhaps be adapted and applied to our modern condition. Amongst ancient superstitions and beliefs, there may have been certain glimmerings of wisdom eclipsed by our present culture. Indeed, in a world not saturated by electromagnetic generation and emissions, in a world not dominated by abstract, urban concepts of 'economy' (an economy that can cut down rain forests in order to supply beef-burger chains with meat), there may have been the practice of a subtle natural science completely overlooked, forgotten as it were, by our brash new world.

For example, the discovery in archaeological excavation of the carefully alternated layers of rock and soil (inorganic and organic layering) in the structure of megalithic mounds such as Knowth in Ireland[3] may have been important. In a completely different context, Wilhelm Reich, an acclaimed student of Freud in his day, felt that boxes made of alternating organic and inorganic layers could accumulate a basic, universal energy he called 'orgone'. He was laughed out of court by establishment science (which is becoming ever more baffled without the useful concept of a universal energy matrix; hence its search for a 'fifth force'). Reich knew nothing of Knowth, but it is a classic example of what he was proposing. Its possible implications have been completely overlooked by the site's investigator, a Professor of Archaeology, because his frame of reference was simply too narrow for him even to consider the possibility of there being a meaning, function or even belief revealed in such layering.

At Knowth and other megalithic mounds in Ireland, it took the brilliant perceptions of artist Martin Brennan to begin to see the function of the carvings, the 'rock art', of those places, a feat not achieved by the archaeologists. Brennan was able to show that the sun at key calendrical times shines into such mounds interacting with the carvings on their stones. He showed the way to the decipherment of some of the glyphs used by the neolithic engineers.[4]

It took another artist, Earth Mysteries researcher John Glover, to discover that the Castlerigg stone circle casts a long shadow into the landscape at midsummer sunset (on a line that links up ancient chapels and holy wells) – a 'shadow path' phenomenon now discovered at other stone circle sites.[5] These – and other – potentially important glimpses of new information about the past is being achieved by Earth Mysteries work, not by archaeologists.

Small or specialist journals in the field of Earth Mysteries are sometimes the first to grasp the significance of new discoveries and observations related to the study of ancient sites. Professor Thom (see below) was given one of his first forums by an 'alternative' publication[6] and the leading Earth Mysteries journal, *The Ley Hunter*,[7] has been first to publish valuable new insights of archaeological relevance. These have included: first account and pictures of the Castlerigg and Long Meg shadow paths mentioned above; publication of the first photographs showing the major lunar standstill at Callanish in 1987; the first report on Martin Brennan's Irish discoveries of light beams interacting with rock carvings; the first published account and photographs of discovered artefacts providing hard evidence for exact prehistoric measure in advance of the archaeological press; the first announcement of the discovery of 'lost' straight Indian tracks in South America by infra-red photography; the first paper on newly discovered sight-lines and astronomical events in the Avebury complex; and other important items.

WEAVING THE WEB

Depending on the amount of research carried out on it, a particular site can become the focus of eight or more strands of research, each apparently a separate study area, yet somehow drawn together by the monument itself. It is as if such places demand a wide-spectrum approach before their *whole* nature can begin to be perceived. Stonehenge has itself not yet been subjected to a fully comprehensive Earth Mysteries investigation, due mainly to difficulty of access because of the unique nature of the site as the country's major prehistoric monument, problems of studying a site attracting massive tourist visitation, passing traffic, and near-by electromagnetic generation for offices, shops and services. An idea of the holistic approach to a site can nevertheless be provided by Stonehenge if we look at a selection of the subject areas encompassed by Earth Mysteries interest.

There is not space here to go into anything in great depth, but an outline can be provided.

The complex archaeology of Stonehenge is referred to elsewhere in the present book, as well as extensively in other works, so is not dealt with here, even though archaeological research is included in the information-gathering processes of Earth Mysteries researchers.

THE ASTRONOMICAL DIMENSION

One of the great modifications to classical archaeological thought has been archaeo-astronomy – the ancient use of astronomy, and the astronomical aspects of prehistoric sites. Stonehenge has been central to this revolution. It was of course known for generations, and noted by the early antiquarians, that the midsummer rising sun could be observed rising over the Heel Stone when viewed from the centre of the sarsen circle. But it was the work of, initially, people like Sir Norman Lockyer at the turn of the century which began the long process of providing the subject with a more scientific basis. The later, more advanced astronomical research at Stonehenge of people like C. A. Newham and Gerald Hawkins showed the structure to have been capable of marking several solar/lunar events and of predicting eclipses. This and other work – above all the far-ranging research of the late Professor Thom at hundreds of megalithic sites in Britain and Brittany generally – has shown that the astronomical dimension of megalithic monuments has to be taken seriously, even if some claims are subject to controversy. Again, this is not the place to enter into a detailed study of archaeo-astronomy, and there are in any case many other sources of this information.[8]

LEYS

We need to spend slightly more space considering the problem of *leys* or *ley lines*, however. This is a major strand of Earth Mysteries work and one of the most controversial – even heretical – in the eyes of establishment archaeology.

Sir Norman Lockyer noted, during his work on Stonehenge, that the henge and the prehistoric earthworks of Old Sarum and Groveley Castle form an equilateral triangle with a side of 9 km (6 miles) (fig. 11). The sides of this triangle could be extended further to align with other ancient sites. The idea of such alignments in the landscape had already been suggested, in different ways, by people such as the Reverend Duke and W. H. Black before Lockyer's day, and researchers like F. J. Bennet and Sir Montague Sharpe who were more or less contemporary with him. But more than anyone else it was Alfred Watkins of Hereford (fig. 12) who, between 1921 and 1935, promoted the observation that certain sites *aligned* across the countryside (fig. 13).[9] Watkins originally called these alignments by the

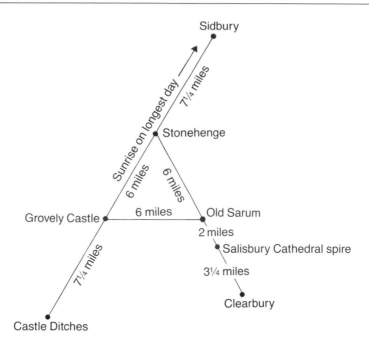

Sidbury

Sunrise on longest day →

7¼ miles

Stonehenge

6 miles

6 miles

Grovely Castle   6 miles   Old Sarum

2 miles

Salisbury Cathedral spire

3¼ miles

Clearbury

7¼ miles

Castle Ditches

11 Sir Norman Lockyer's terrestrial triangle formed by Stonehenge, Grovely Castle, and Old Sarum.

Saxon term 'leys' for various etymological reasons it is not necessary to explore here; he abandoned the word a few years before his death.[10] He felt they were the remnants of straight traders' routes originally laid down in the Neolithic period and subsequently modified until they were eventually forgotten about during the historical period. Their existence was therefore only recordable by the positioning of prehistoric sites along these 'old straight tracks', and by the evolved continuation of some otherwise obliterated prehistoric sites into the historic period by means, for example, of the Christianization of a site by the erection of a church or cross on it (fig. 14). In other words, the ley alignments themselves were as much ruins as were the stone and earth monuments of the same period.

This modest observation caused outrage amongst orthodox archaeologists of Watkins' day, and the archaeological journal *Antiquity* even refused an advert for his main book on the subject, *The Old Straight Track*. Undaunted, Watkins and his followers continued their researches into these ancient alignments in the pre-Second World War years, while, unknown to them, similar work on *Heilige Linien* ('holy lines') was being carried out by people like Teudt and Heinsch in Germany during the same period. The Second World War put an end to that period of the subject, but there was a major revival of interest in Watkins' work in the 1960s which has been maintained to the present day.

12 Alfred Watkins, the discoverer of leys, shown here with his camera, recording an alignment.
Photograph by Major Tyler.

13 Part of one of Alfred Watkins's leys in the Black Mountains on the Welsh border. The course of the alignment, which passes through Llanthony Abbey, is marked for part of its course by an ancient 'hollow' road (foreground). Lines on the alignment can be discerned going straight up the side of the far hill.
Photograph by Paul Devereux.

14 A Christianized dolmen in Carnac-Ville, Brittany.
Photograph by Paul Devereux.

The puzzle presented by straight ancient linear features is considerable, and
Earth Mysteries researchers know that unless this early practice can be
understood, a fundamental principle of a former geomantic system will remain
unknown; that we will have forgotten some knowledge or belief basic to the
thinking of early pre-industrial peoples in Britain and elsewhere (fig. 15). We will
have failed to hear the archaic whisper from our landscape. The delicate evidence
of ancient alignments, still just discernible on the land, will be wasted.

Those who study ancient alignments are popularly known as 'ley hunters', and
they form one of the main factions of alternative researchers. While there is not
space here to discuss properly the current position regarding the status of these ley
alignments, a few points can be briefly mentioned.

The very idea of old straight tracks was thought ludicrous in Watkins' day.
Now, of course, we know better. In the Andes dead straight tracks have been
found, the best-known probably being those at Nasca in Peru.[11] But the old
straight tracks in the *altiplano* of Bolivia are even more impressive, and are in
every way identical to Watkins' concept of leys, even to the fact that some Indian
sites on these holy tracks, or *t'akis*, have been Christianized with Spanish
churches or adobe shrines.[12] Alignments known as *ceques* radiated out from the
Inca Temple of the Sun in Cuzco, Peru; until recently these were marked only by

15 This example of leys is in Marietta, Ohio, USA, where the citizens preserved the course of a 2000-year-old Indian ceremonial road which ran straight from the Muskingum River to an earthwork. It is now called 'Sacra Via'.
Photograph by Paul Devereux.

the alignment of Indian sites, exactly like leys in Britain, but Tony Morrison has recently been able to photograph these straight lines by means of infra-red photography.[13] Versions of straight-line geomancy are known and proved beyond any doubt whatsoever in other parts of the world – in China, Indonesia, and even the USA, where arrow-straight prehistoric Indian tracks running for many miles are known in the Californian sierras, in Colorado, Nevada, and New Mexico. These are 'leys' in every respect.[14]

In Britain however, there remains considerable scepticism, in spite of the remarkable coincidence that Watkins' ideas so closely prefigured these later findings in other parts of the world.

One complaint has been that Watkins' leys incorporate marker sites of mixed dates – say a stone circle of 1700 BC on the same line as a church of AD 1100. In fact, examples of claimed leys exist which are marked by archaeologically homo-geneous sites, i.e., sites on the line are from the same time period, such the extension by John Michell's (fig. 16) of Lockyer's Bronze Age Cornish megalithic alignments[15] or the linear relationships between the Neolithic Devil's Arrows standing stones and henge monuments in Yorkshire.[16] In the other, mixed-marker cases, Watkins argued that later features, such as pre-Reformation churches, were the result of *site evolution*. It is certainly true that Christianization

16 John Michell, *doyen* of ley hunters, at Stonehenge. Behind him rises the bulk of the Heel Stone, an essential element in Stonehenge geometry.
Photograph by Christopher Chippindale.

17 Looking south down the Stonehenge – Old Sarum ley. Old Sarum in the foreground, Salisbury Cathedral in the middle distance, and Clearbury Ring, covered by a clump of trees, on the horizon. This version of the ley passes through the east, altar end, of the cathedral. The street grid of Salisbury aligns on this ley. *Photograph by Paul Devereux.*

of earlier sites was widely practised by the Church.[17] A typical example of a mixed-marker ley is a version of one of Lockyer's original alignments, going south from Stonehenge and on through Old Sarum, Salisbury Cathedral, Clearbury Ring and, in an extended version, to Frankenbury Camp (fig. 17).[18] (Salisbury Cathedral is recorded in folklore as being founded as the result of a vision or where an arrow fell – both methods used in former traditional placing procedures.)

Another major criticism of the ley theory is the claim that the lines are due to the chance lining up of sites; that they are not deliberate, surveyed features. In fact, the best statistical work to date has shown a good proportion of individual ley alignments so analysed to be statistically significant (fig. 18). At the present time, however, improved statistical techniques are being tried out, and we have to await their results. The main disadvantage of statistics is that not all the information on an alignment can be used; it has to be abstracted for mathematical modelling. Also, it is arguable whether deliberate alignments would necessarily show up statistically in certain areas where, for example, there has been a large amount of later activity by cultures not using alignment practices. Nevertheless, statistical appraisal of leys is welcomed by ley hunters as of some use.

No other criticisms of the ley principle have been shown to be fundamental, relevant or valid. Orthodox archaeology has been slow to realize that a potentially important aspect of prehistory is being unveiled by alternative research. Only one archaeologist, Tom Williamson, has seriously attempted to challenge ley work, in a book called *Ley lines in question*[19] written with Liz Bellamy. While some valid criticisms of ley theory were made in the book, nothing fatal to the basic case for leys was presented, and much of their argument was flawed by being poorly informed, muddled and out of date.

The ley theory cannot be either proven or disproven as yet, but strong evidence exists to support at least a part of Watkins' original ideas. The question of leys is somewhat confused, however, by claims that the alignments mark lines of some form of terrestrial current. Here, I am simply putting forward leys as alignments of sites. The idea that they mark the course of some unknown energy comes from occult and dowsing sources since the death of Watkins, and remains unproven outside of those fields. Personally, I have an open mind but would want to see other than subjective evidence. *Claims that leys are energy lines is a relatively recent addition to ley theory, and is not derived from core ley research.*

There may not be energies racing cross the countryside in straight lines, but it is crucial for us not to forget that ancient peoples worldwide believed *spirits* did so. Cultures as widespread as the Aymara Indians of South America, the temple builders of Indonesia, the *feng shui* geomants of China and Irish peasants agreed that straight lines in the landscape allowed the passage of spirits of one kind or another. This aspect of leys as traditional spirit lines is dealt with in work recently published.[20]

18 Tallest of the three monoliths known as the Devil's Arrows, near Boroughbridge, Yorkshire. Two alignments radiating from here, and incorporating only other Neolithic sites, have been shown in the latest, most sophisticated statistical studies to have beaten simulated alignments in 400 computer runs.
Photograph by Paul Devereux.

Research has also uncovered the fact that Stonehenge is a key site in opening up a deeper understanding of alignments in the ancient British landscape – the old geomantic site doing its job again. Quite apart from the alignments through the site noted by Lockyer and later by Watkins, the Stonehenge landscape offers a more archaeologically secure example of alignment concepts on the part of Neolithic peoples. If the visitor to Stonehenge follows the track off the A344 immediately by the western end of the car park, he will encounter National Trust signs that mark the course of a *cursus*. This feature was discovered by the antiquarian William Stukeley in 1723. Due to the depredations of forestry and the plough, it is now a much-damaged monument compared to its condition in Stukeley's time, and can scarcely be discerned from ground level. The cursus is a linear enclosure over 3000 m (9700 ft) long, marked by the remnants of two banks and ditches 110 m (350 ft) or more apart. At its western end (in Fargo Plantation) earthen mounds are enclosed by the terminating ditch. The eastern end has now disappeared along with a long barrow that was immediately adjacent to it, set almost at right angles to the course of the cursus. Archaeologist R. J. C. Atkinson admitted that the cursus had been 'deliberately aligned' to the barrow.[21]

Stukeley thought this linear enclosure was an ancient British racecourse, hence the name *cursus* (Latin for racecourse) that he gave it, but this huge Neolithic linear feature remains a mystery. In 1947, archaeologist J. F. S. Stone made the observation that the *cursus*' axis, 'if projected 1500 yards to the east, strikes Woodhenge and passes the Cuckoo or Cuckold Stone by the way'.[22] Stone could have been more specific; the northern ditch of the *cursus*, dead straight for almost its entire length, aligns through the Cuckoo Stone and on to the central area of Woodhenge (figs. 19, 20). This straight earthwork, standing stone and circular monument form an alignment over 4 km (2½ miles) long. This *geographical* dimension or extension to the *cursus* is crucial; the alignment, marked on the

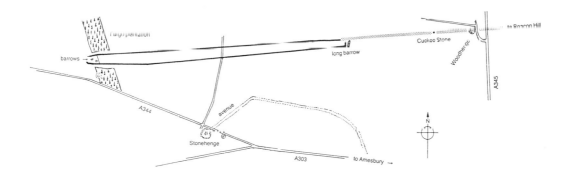

19 The Stonehenge Cursus ley.

20 The Cuckoo or Cuckold Stone, to the east of the Stonehenge Cursus and on the extended axis of its northern ditch. In every way this fallen megalith served the purpose of one of Alfred Watkin's 'ley markers'.
Photograph by Paul Devereux.

ground for well over half its length, *is* a ley. In her 1959 excavations, Patricia Christie found some evidence to suggest that the northern ditch was dug first, with the southern one being made some time later.[23] Looking at the cursus, it certainly seems to be the case that it is the northern ditch which was surveyed, with the southern ditch being ranged out from that. This could account for the varying width of the *cursus*. This alignment certainly did not happen casually or by chance, for Woodhenge is not visible from the cursus. It was a deliberate piece of planned aligning involving considerable effort. This did not happen in a cultural vacuum, and must be understood as an example of some linear impulse of the period that has fortunately survived because of the relatively well-preserved status of the ritual landscape around Stonehenge. Finally, the axis of the cursus extends beyond Woodhenge to Beacon Hill, and beacon hills were considered by Alfred Watkins to be classic 'initial points' on leys.

About 50 confirmed or suspected *cursuses* have now been identified around Britain. They are amongst the largest and most ancient monuments left in the British landscape, and yet hardly known by the general public, nor yet properly addressed by the archaeological community – though increasing attention is now being paid to them. This is partly because they are usually visible from the air only as crop markings, and their purpose is obscure to modern thought. Because of (now largely outdated) prejudices against ley theory, archaeologists have conceptually blinded themselves regarding geographical extensions of these cursuses. There is a kind of intellectual quarantine surrounding the subject of prehistoric alignment practice. Just here and there in the archaeological literature are tentative references to alignment made. It may be some time before archaeology realizes that in these almost vanished monuments we have the record of archaic linear practices that does more to support the ley hunters' stance than it

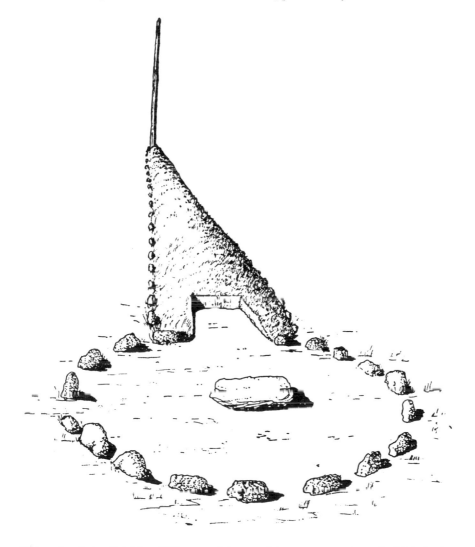

21 The axis of the Crickley Hill mound (a possible reconstruction of which is shown here) visually aligns to the spot now marked by Gloucester cathedral. *Photograph by Paul Devereux.*

22 Part of a Dartmoor Bronze Age boundary or 'reave', running straight for miles across Walkhampton Common.
Photograph by Paul Devereux.

does to comfort their detractors (figs. 21, 22). It may be left to Earth Mysteries research to highlight this situation. It was left to Stonehenge to be the catalyst.

Ley hunters have, however, also conceptually restricted themselves. When finding leys in cities comprised of alignments of churches, for example, they have automatically assumed that all the churches marking the lines must be standing on the spot of former prehistoric sites. While this unquestionably does happen (and probably more frequently than archaeologists are prepared to accept), it has been a ley-hunting error to think of all alignments as conforming to a prehistoric pattern, or even as relating to a single scheme. Research by Nigel Pennick, Brian Larkman, Pat McFadzean and others is uncovering medieval church alignment schemes[24] and is drawing attention to the nature and origins of ancient city grids and boundaries. The word 'ley' covers a number of (not necessarily directly related) alignment schemes, and it is only now that ley research is beginning to untangle the mess. But site-aligning in the Neolithic landscape was certainly one aspect of a prehistoric British geomancy. *It is quite possible that the widespread ancient idea of spirits travelling in straight lines has a bearing on the function of cursuses in Neolithic times.*

MEASURE

Another strand of enquiry woven around (or perhaps by) ancient sites is that of *measures* being used at them. Perhaps the most victimized monument in this respect has been the Great Pyramid at Giza, about which all kinds of fatuous measurements and proportions have been claimed. That does not mean, of course, that *all* such observations are erroneous or without significance. Stonehenge likewise has been the butt of many metrological fancies. The best work of this kind, however, has been carried out by John Michell.[25] With meticulous scholarship he has been able to demonstrate that the proportions of Stonehenge encode the measures of the Earth. Viewed in this way, one of the functions of Stonehenge would seem to have been to serve as a vast mnemonic device fashioned out of carefully shaped and placed stones: a storehouse of ancient knowledge of time and space, a 'permanent repository of standards' as Michell has put it, which could be ritually activated. While some people tend to deride ancient metrological studies, and to complain, with some justification, that 'numbers can be read into anything', it is important not to throw the baby out with the bathwater. Stonehenge was laid out with unimaginable skill and care, considering the technology available to fashion it. It clearly *does* demonstrate a concern with ground-plan and proportional (space) accuracy. It *does* contain evidence that astronomical (time) measurements could be made with it. It would be unwise in the extreme to dismiss the implication of these facts simply because it does not fit in with the prejudices of twentieth-century thinking. Such dismissal would also be unscientific, because Michell has shown that the measurements are there in the fabric of Stonehenge. *They are there.*

LORE

Another aspect of study the old places draw in around themselves is folklore. Traditions associated with Stonehenge include the beliefs that the bluestones were brought from Ireland by Merlin,[26] that all the stones in the structure possess healing properties, that the stones were the dancing ground for giants (or were giants petrified in the act of dancing), and that the stones of the monument cannot be counted correctly.[27] With the exception of the Merlin tradition, these legends are typical of the folklore attending many other prehistoric sites. The following are basic legendary motifs to be found variously associated with numerous monuments:

- Stones have healing properties.
- Stones can move (usually at midnight or dawn) e.g. going for a drink from a near-by stream, or running around their field.
- Stones or earthworks will bring bad luck or storms if desecrated.
- Stones or earthworks are the abode of faeries and nature spirits; some are places of enchantment (time anomaly).
- Stones are petrified people (usually for transgressing the sabbath).
- Stones in a circle cannot be counted.
- Stones were hurled to their present position by a giant (or the Devil).
- Stones and earthworks contain or conceal treasure.

Some of the same motifs are found associated with standing stones in cultures as diverse as the British Isles and the Senegambian region of West Africa.

There are many other, less major, traditions, to do with music and lights emanating from sites, underground tunnels, King Arthur, number mysticism, Christianization, the use of stones for divination or the making of contracts, and so on. The imagery of such legends clearly owes a great deal to story-telling down many generations of huddling around rural hearths. Earth Mysteries researchers feel that some of the motifs could, however, contain fragments of information that have been preserved for millennia in a legendary matrix, like oral time-capsules. For example, traditions of stones being able to heal might possibly relate to sporadic and minute electromagnetic effects occurring in and around megaliths. Many of the healing legends relate to the curing of bone disorders; mild electromagnetic therapy is now employed by modern medicine for treating just such ailments. We should not dismiss too readily the experience of many generations of country folk who have shared the landscape with the ancient places. They, after all, have had the most intimate knowledge of them. In any case, as will be seen below, there have recently been definite, instrumental measurements of geomagnetic variations in megaliths that make such ideas less fanciful now than may once have been the case.

ENERGIES

In 1977 a part-time, unofficial research programme called the Dragon Project was formed as part of the Earth Mysteries effort to investigate the rumour of energies at megalithic British sites. It uses both primary sensing techniques and also scientific, instrumental monitoring of sites. The lack of resources experienced by the Project – operating as it does outside the normal channels of funding such as universities or official research grants, conducting controversial research, relying on volunteer workers, goodwill and intermittent private donations – has made progress slow. The Project is thus still on-going, and will be for years to come (fig. 23). It was made into the Dragon Project Trust in December 1987.[28]

It is impossible here even to attempt to describe this work properly, and only a nominal outline can be given. But it can be clearly stated that geomagnetic behaviour at certain megalithic sites in England and Wales has now quite definitely been recorded by the investigations of the Dragon Project and two other independent studies (fig. 24).[29]

It may seem ludicrous to the classically-trained archaeologist that alternative researchers bother with such investigations, but as the work of Dr Robin Baker at the University of Manchester has shown,[30] there are centres in human beings that may make us sensitive to the Earth's magnetic field, as other organisms are known to be.[31] Magnetic sensitivity in humans may be related to iron dumping in the body from food. The more robust diet of Neolithic people may have contained greater iron content, thus allowing more iron dumping and thus greater magnetic sensitivity. Even some modern humans have been measured as sensitive to a thousandth of a gauss – a very small unit of magnetic field strength.

It is possible that the megalithic builders could sense a magnetic anomaly in a stone directly, and consider it important for their purposes – be they religious or a form of instinctual, natural science. Certainly, the latest Earth Mysteries research is discovering magnetic effects from megaliths sufficiently strong that magnetometers are not required to detect it – compass disturbance at specific stones at sites is being increasingly noted. (The use of magnetite, the old lodestone, could also have been employed by the megalith builders to detect magnetic stones. The lodestone is known to have been in use at least as far back as ancient Greece.)

Magnetic research is, in fact, the only kind of Dragon Project work to have yet been carried out at Stonehenge. Tests were conducted in September 1987 on some of the bluestones, as a result of findings on the Preseli Hills in south Wales (fig. 25). This work showed no magnetic anomalies, but Paul McCartney, a geologist working with the Dragon Project, felt strongly that the Stonehenge bluestones may not, in fact, originate from the supposed Preseli origination locations he had

23 A dowser using angle rods and being monitored by an EEG device at the Rollright Stones, Oxfordshire, during a Dragon Project research session.
Photograph by Paul Devereux.

24 The 14-feet tall Llangynidr Stone, near Crickhowell, Wales. This was the first standing stone to be tested by scientists for geophysical anomalies. *Photograph by Paul Devereux.*

been studying. This opinion was later supported (personal comment) by archaeologist Michael Pitts, who conducted excavations at Stonehenge in 1979/80. It may be that the Dragon Project has inadvertently drawn attention to a problem relating to the origin of the Stonehenge bluestones.

In addition to magnetic effects, the Dragon Project and related research has uncovered puzzling anomalies with regard to natural radiation, ultrasound, radio propagation and other energetic effects at various sites, particularly at the Project's field-base site of the Rollright circle (figs. 26, 27), but such work has not yet been carried out at Stonehenge.

The Belgian researcher Pierre Méraux has shown that some of the groupings of stone rows at Carnac, Brittany, approximate to the boundaries of gravity anomalies.[32] It has also been found that Carnac rows, like British stone circles (not henges), are geographically coincidental with geological faulting or associated tectonic intrusions. These types of landscape are especially prone to the appearance of unexplained aerial light phenomena – which some people call 'UFOs' and consider to be spaceships from another world. Although early Earth Mysteries enthusiasts made lurid claims in the 1960s concerning supposed connections between ancient sites and UFOs, this simplistic notion has long been

25 Dragon Project volunteers setting up magnetic tests at the Stonehenge bluestones (the shorter megaliths) in September 1987.
Photograph by Paul Devereux.

superseded by more mature Earth Mysteries work, even though the old, over-enthusiastic ideas are still trotted out occasionally by journalistic hacks. The psychedelic notions of the early Earth Mysteries researchers may, however, have been right in a sense, if for the wrong reasons. Current Earth Mysteries research, and the research of certain geologists, is now clearly demonstrating that such lights are almost certainly a form of hitherto uninvestigated natural energy generated by geological conditions at certain times and places.[33] The forces that give rise to such phenomena may also have attracted the megalith builders, if they were sensitive in a primary manner to energy effects in the ground and atmosphere of the electromagnetically pristine Neolithic and early Bronze Age environment. Certainly, a body of responsible eyewitness testimony is currently being built up concerning light effects at quite a number of megalithic sites around Britain – and, indeed, light phenomena have been reported at Stonehenge itself.

In the way that chemistry (through dating techniques), geology (through petrological studies of artefacts), engineering (through surveying and the study of possible megalithic building methods) and astronomy have had their impact on archaeology, it may be the case that archaeology will have to take into account a wider range of geophysical properties than hitherto at certain prehistoric sites.

26 Monitoring background radiation at a megalithic site during a Dragon Project session.
Photograph by Paul Devereux.

27 Testing for infra-red emissions at the Kingstone, Rollright. This stone, a location near the Rollright Circle, and Kit's Coty house dolmen in Kent, have all yielded unexplained effects on infra-red film.
Photograph by Graham Challifour.

28 Paul Devereux with twin magnetometers monitoring stone and environment magnetic field variations at the Kermario stone row, Carnac, Brittany, as part of the Dragon Project.
Photograph by Jeanne Sheridan.

One day, perhaps, archaeology will expand to the inclusive approach of Earth Mysteries research in spite of itself. But however that might turn out, Stonehenge will continue to bear witness – wiser than any of us (fig. 28).

CHAPTER THREE

SYLWADAU CYNFRODOR
AR GÔR Y CEWRI;

Rhys Jones

or a British Aboriginal's land claim to Stonehenge

The period may arrive when New Zealand may produce her Lockes, her Newtons, and her Montesquieus; and when great nations in the immense region of New Holland, may send their navigators, philosophers, and antiquaries, to contemplate the ruins of *ancient* London and Paris, and to trace the languid remains of the arts and sciences in this quarter of the globe.

JOHN STOCKDALE (1800)

It is in the nature of land claims that they depend on antiquity, on a history of living on the land that has been taken away. 'This land is our land,' say Aboriginal Australians, and it has been the land of their ancestors since the Dreamtime or, in the white man's way of saying it, since at least 30,000 years ago. So my land claim to Stonehenge, the greatest work of Aboriginal Britons, depends on the most ancient history of Britain as it has been remembered, recovered or reconstructed.

'Côr y Cewri' we Welsh call it – 'Court of the Giants', that hulking mass of stones that the English call 'Stonehenge'. Our word is old. It is recorded in the thirteenth-century Bruts and in the Red Book of Hergest that codify a rich oral tradition extending back to a time just after the collapse of the Roman Empire. The language of the Bruts is *Cymraeg*, the people *Y Cymry*, derived from the old British *Combrogi* – 'fellow countrymen'; those whom the invading Saxons called 'Welsh' or foreigners.

The usual Welsh word for a megalithic monument is *cromlech*, like *cromlegh* in Old Cornish and *kroumlec'h* in Breton (fig. 29). The Peniarth medieval manuscripts say the new palace of the bishop of Llan Elwy (St Asaph) was '*yn ymyl y gromlech*', 'near the cromlech'. A letter to Edward Lhuyd in 1693 from John Davies, the Rector of Newburgh in Anglesey, explains the word in describing the monument at Bod Owyr on the island:

> composed of three or four rude stones, or more, pitched on end as supporters or pillars, and a vast stone of several tuns laid on them as a covering; and are

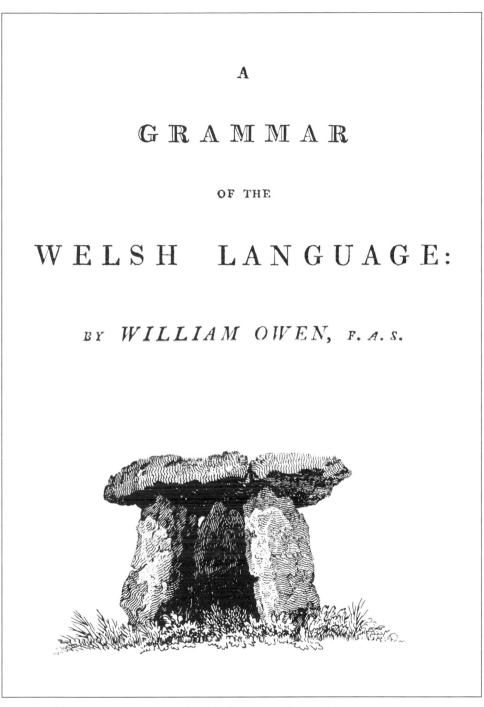

A

GRAMMAR

OF THE

WELSH LANGUAGE:

BY *WILLIAM OWEN*, F. A. S.

29 A Welsh *cromlech* of the smaller kind makes a fitting titlepage decoration to William Owen's pioneering eighteenth-century *Grammar of the Welsh language*.

30 The Pentre Ifan megalith, a grander emblem of Welsh antiquity, in a view of 1835, by Richard Tongue.
Courtesy of the Society of Antiquaries of London.

thought to have received the name of *Cromlechau*, for that the Table or covering stone is on the upper side somewhat gibbous or convex: the word *Krwm* signifying . . . crooked or hunch-back'd, and *Llech* any flat stone.

The Welsh word *maen*, often associated with the names of individual monuments, means a large block of stone, especially one that has been hewn or worked. *Cist-faen*, 'chest or coffer of stone', was often used by Lhuyd in his field notes for what modern archaeologists call chambered tombs. The Breton *men* is in *dolmen* and *menhir* or 'long stone' – essential words for any megalithic buff.

The famous site of Pentre Ifan high on the slopes of the Preseli Mountains in south-west Wales appears in George Owen of Henllys's *Description of Penbrockshire* in 1603, as 'the stone called Maen y gromlegh upon Pentre Jevan lande'. Richard Tongue's oil painting of 1835 (fig. 30) shows four vertical stones capped by a massive cap-stone, slightly tilted, and balanced delicately on the tips of three uprights. Behind is a 'sublime' vista of moorland and mountain. The mood is sombre, even ominous. Below the cromlech sits a countryman with rustic straw hat and stick, head down, body slumped, as if in uncomprehending awe of the mute and ancient mysteries. The same theme is used by Henry Hodges, artist on Cook's second voyage to the Pacific in 1774–5, whose view of Easter Island (fig. 31) places the time-gnarled monoliths with their red pumice top-stones, some standing and some in archaic collapse, opposite a mass of natural rocks, fecund with vegetation. At the base of a rock ledge are parts of a human skeleton, half scattered on the strand; behind is a back-drop of the sea. A man leans against a spear or staff, a breadfruit in his right hand, oblivious to the great statues behind him. He cannot comprehend those relics of a lost age, and lives off the easy products of a bountiful nature, untroubled by effort and industry.

Hodges's teacher was the Welsh painter Richard Wilson, from Penegoes in Montgomeryshire, who himself had wandered along the same path. In '*Ego Fui in Arcadia*' ('I too once lived in Arcadia'), painted in Italy in 1755, Wilson set two shepherds in front of a fallen mass of Classical columns and of engraved stone slabs. One leans on his staff like Hodges's Easter Island man and Tongue's Welsh yokel.

An old theme in pastoral art is a longing for a past Golden Age, when people were integrated with bountiful nature, or climbed to some high culture. Now, they have become carefree, simple and – unfortunately – ignorant. The Golden

31 Henry Hodges engraving of Easter Island monoliths, after drawing of 1774–5.

Age becomes part of a history that can never be brought back to life; only the ruined monuments of past glories survive to strike some mute, half-comprehended chord of memory.

In the Welsh view of our past, the stone monuments have a special place. It is the *cromlechau* and the stone circles that have been taken to stand for that past age, especially the stone circles, the class of ancient site of which Stonehenge is the grandest and the most polite – more polished by far than the ruder megaliths of our hills. It is a stone circle that we have chosen to build each year for the annual festival that celebrates our cultural survival.

My own middle name is Maengwyn, which was also my father's. The family, when they moved from rural Meirionydd and Maldwyn into the maws of the industrial towns, named their children after important totemic sites of their own *bro* or country. Some were wells of early Celtic saints, others were mythical sites. It was my luck to be named after the megalithic monument of Ynys y Maengwyn – literally 'Island of the white, shining or magical stone' situated in south-west Meirion in the sand dunes north of the Dyfi estuary. Not every archaeologist has the good fortune to be named after a megalith; it makes an excellent start for my land claim.

THE LOST WORLDS OF BRITAIN

Cenedl heb iaith, Cenedl heb gof is a Welsh adage: a nation without a language is one without a memory. Many of the oldest Welsh poems tell of battles against invaders; Angles and Saxons from the south and east, Picts from the north, and Goidels from Ireland. In the sixth century AD a form of Welsh was the language of wide areas of western Britain, from Cornwall through Wales and part of present-day Hereford and Shropshire into northern England and southern Scotland (fig. 32). These are the lost lands of Wales. A Welsh-speaking land corridor, tenuously held but still contiguous, linked the north British and western regions. In south Scotland, there were three kingdoms – Gododdin centred around Edinburgh, then called Din Eidyn (*cf.* Dunedin), Rheged around the Solway with Carlisle as its capital, and Ystrad Glud or Strathclyde around Dumbarton and Glasgow. This was the western and northern heartland of the earliest Welsh poems, in the regions less corrupted by the centuries of Roman occupation.

The truth is that we lost all of these lands; we were reduced finally to the mountainous peninsulae of the west. Old Ystrad Glud (Strathclyde) held on until the eleventh century, its Cymraeg literary traditions crucial to the survival of the north British poems. In Cumberland (cf. Combrogi = Cymry), the shepherds use a remnant of the old language in their duo-decimal counting system for sheep: *deugain, trigain, pedwar ugain* – what the French call *quatre vingt and cant*. The

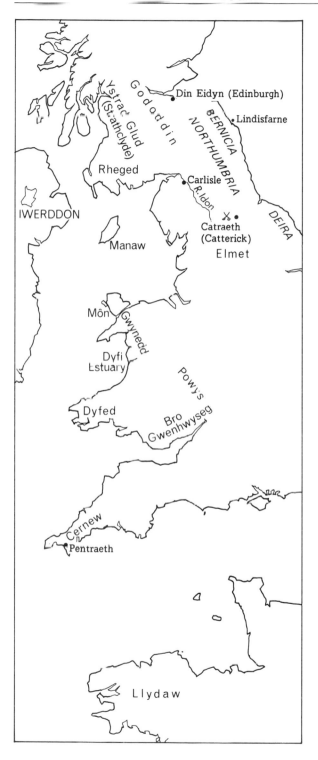

32 The lost lands of Wales.

Brut of the Princes in the Red Book of Hergest describes the stark and inescapable facts in its first lines:

Pedwar ugain a chwech chant oedd oed Crist pan fu farwolaeth fawr drwy holl ynys Prydain. . .

Six hundred and eighty was the year of Christ when there was a great mortality throughout the island of Britain. And from the beginning of the world till then, there was one year short of five thousand eight hundred and eighty years. . .

With that, we Britons were forced off the land that was ours:

Ac o hyny allan y colles y Brytanyiet goron y deyrnas; ac yd ennillawd y Saesson hi.

And from that time forth, the Britons lost the crown of the kingdom and the Saxons won it.

Y BEIRDD

We call the early poets Taliesin and Aneirin the *cynfeirdd*, the 'earliest' or 'proto' bards.

The old Celtic word for a poet was *bardos*, from which the Welsh *bardd* (plural – *beirdd*) and the Irish *bard* were derived. The word 'bard' in English is now a patronizing term, with a hint of rustic or antique irrelevance not accorded to the word 'poet'. Although 'poet' is part of its meaning, the word *bardd* has other connotations, both historically and also in modern Welsh life. I will therefore use the uncorrupted term *bardd*. At the dawn of our language, the *beirdd* were the holders of the oral traditions, mnemonics for the genealogies of lordly patrilines, and they praised their deeds. Some *beirdd* were believed to have magical powers in remembering ancient events and foretelling future ones.

Several classical sources, including Diodorus Siculus, Caesar and Strabo, refer to three intellectual classes within the society of Celtic Gaul: *bardoi* ('bards'), *vates* or *manteis* ('seers'), and *druidai* or *druides* ('druids'). Modern scholars believe the *druidai* were the 'leading professional learned class in Gaul who, to some extent, may have fulfilled priestly and judicial functions'.[1] They did not survive Romanization and disappear from history until resurrected by the fanciful theories of antiquarians. But the *beirdd* had a vital role in the Welsh and Irish societies that emerged after the decline of Rome. They were integral to intellectual and political life in Dark Age and early medieval Welsh society, carrying historical traditions through to their recording in written form.

Whereas monuments of the past do not speak, poetry gives them life. With the *awen*, the inspiration of spirit, the rustic survivor from the Golden Age does not stare at the ruins with mute ignorance.

How often have I, as archaeologist, organized my own records in the same way; site number *x*, quadrant *y*, grid reference *z*, type *A*, significance level *B*; a compilation of meticulous facts devoid of cultural meaning; the objective yokel, blind and uncomprehending before the monument.

That the sense of 'ownership' of the past carries with it powerful political implications has long been a theme of Welsh history; it is a predilection of all small nations swallowed up by larger polities.

GEOFFREY AND THE STORY OF WALES

Geoffrey of Monmouth wrote his highly influential *Historia Regum Britanniae*, The History of the Kings of Britain, at Oxford in 1136. Although he came from the Norman ruling class and was later Bishop Elect of St Asaph on the then English–Gwynedd military frontier, Geoffrey says in a telling little phrase that he is *pudibundus Brito* – 'an abashed Briton'. He may have been referring to a Welsh, or to a Breton or Cornish ancestry. His 'History' traced an unbroken lineage for the ancestors of his British countrymen from Cadwallader, who finally lost Britain to the Saxons, back through a heroic age of Arthur and the prophet Merlin, beyond the Romans to a distant ancestry 1200 years before Christ, when Brutus, great-grandson of Aeneas of Troy, had landed on the island to which he gave his name – Britain – with his son Camber – Cymru. To Geoffrey's contemporary Welsh readers, it told an extra, powerful message: although incapable of resisting Norman arms, they had a charter, an unbroken history on their own land, which rivalled the antiquity of Rome itself. The Latin *Historia*, quickly translated into Welsh as *Brut y Brenhinoedd*, was embedded into Welsh historical and literary consciousness.

Among many tales Geoffrey's History related the victory of the saintly Aurelius Ambrosius (Emrys) the 'Armorican Briton' (Breton), over the pagan Saxon, Hengist, who previously had defeated the 'island Britons', of whom he had 'the lowest possible opinion'. Aurelius, that man literally from the golden age, wishing to erect a 'novel building' to commemorate the worthies killed by the Saxons at Kaercaradduc (Salisbury), went to near-by 'Mount Ambrius'. There Aurelius collected together the carpenters and stone masons to plan a fitting memorial; 'the whole band racked their brains and then confessed themselves beaten'. The wizard Merlin broke the *impasse* by suggesting a suitable and lasting monument:

> Send for the Giant's Ring which is on Mount Killaraus in Ireland. In that place is a stone construction which no man of this period could ever erect. . . . The stones are enormous and there is no one alive strong enough to move them . . . they will stand for ever. . . . These stones are connected with certain secret religious rites and they have various properties which are medicinally important. Many years ago, the Giants transported them from the remotest

confines of Africa and set them up in Ireland at a time when they inhabited that country.

The men of Ireland, hearing that an army of 15,000 Britons – a sort of militarized Lord Elgin – were about to descend to take away their ancient monuments, massed in response, but were beaten, their leader saying, 'Surely the stones of Ireland aren't so much better than those of Britain that our realm has to be invaded for their sake?'

The Irish were defeated, but the British, try as they must, were not able to dismantle the stone ring. 'They rigged up hawsers and ropes and they propped up scaling-ladders, each preparing what he thought most useful, but none of these things advanced them an inch.' Merlin, laughing, used his magical power, and 'dismantled the stones more easily that you could ever believe'. They were taken over to Mount Ambrius, where:

> Merlin obeyed the King's order and put the stones up in a circle round the sepulchre, in exactly the same way as they had been arranged on Mount Killaraus in Ireland, thus proving that his artistry was worth more than any brute strength.

It is this very monument, brought from Ireland by the artistry of magical means, which is Stonehenge.

Here is a medieval myth about the very origin of Stonehenge itself. Already it knows its prior British association, and control over its supernatural powers is in the firm hands of a British magician.

UNION WITH ENGLAND

At Bosworth Field in 1485, Henry Tudor unfurled the Red Dragon flag of Cadwallader. This final resolution of the Wars of the Roses destroyed the separate unity of the Welsh upper class, the *Uchelwyr* ('high people'), as no punitive expedition had ever done. The Seisyllts of the Welsh-speaking part of Herefordshire anglicized their name to Cecil and became powerful in Elizabeth's court. The buccaneer and poet Tomos Prys of Plas Iolyn wrote strict-metre *cywyddau* about fighting in Flanders and raiding Spanish shipping:

Drac a hwyliodd, draig helynt,
Amgylch y byd i gyd gynt.

Drake sailed, dragon of trouble,
Around all the world once.

The Act of Union of 1536 was designed 'utterly to extirpe all and singular the senister usages and customes differing from [the Realme of Englande]' – all separate customs, legal systems and regional government. In particular, the Act stated, the Welsh people 'do daily use a speche nothing like nor consonant to the natural Mother tongue used within [the] realm'. So Welsh was barred from all legal and official functions: 'no person . . . that use Welsh speech . . . shall have . . . office or fees within this realm . . . unless he . . . use and excercise the English speech or tongue'.

Two formal *eisteddfodau* were held under Royal patronage in the north-east Welsh town of Caerwys in 1523 and 1567. The *eisteddfod*, literally 'session', was a genuine Welsh institution, where poets and musicians met in competition for prizes and honours. And an *eisteddfod* provided the means to license the poets who were skilled in formal metres (and permitted to continue the craft), while

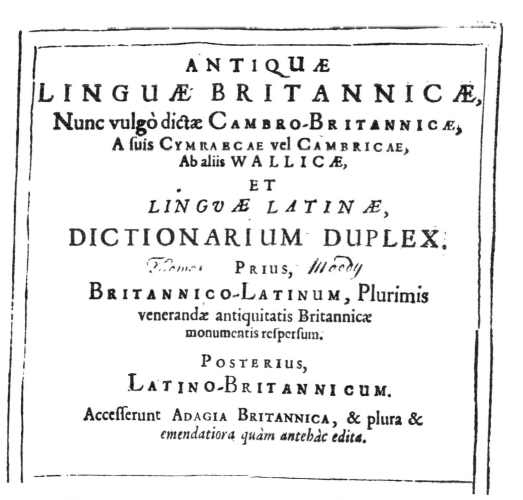

33 Detail from the titlepage of the *Dictionarium Duplex*, by John Davies of Mallwyd. Its two languages were the great old tongues, British [i.e. Welsh] and Latin.

others were condemned as vagabonds; the Council of Wales noted in 1567 with disgust 'an intolerable multitude' of 'vagrant and idle persons naming themselves minstrels, rhymers and bards'. The Caerwys *eisteddfodau* also had a political function, in registering and therefore controlling the *beirdd* and their politically significant message. A separate, scholarly purpose, the codifying and making-explicit of the various traditional metres, stemmed partly from a humanist concern that the grammatical and poetical rules of Welsh should be consistent with those of Latin and the Classical traditions.

The great social and economic changes of the new English Renaissance mercantile state put the whole structure of traditional Welsh society into collapse. The old, irrelevant learning was lost, consigned to manuscript libraries in country houses. Welsh culture and history took on the appearance of rustic quaintness or even cultural backwardness – the Taffys of the hills, the bawdy rhymsters in taverns, the little rituals at the passing of the seasons.

As for the Welsh language, the

> Native Gibberish . . . usually prattled throughout the whole Taphydome, except in their Market Towns whose Inhabitants being a little rais'd . . . do begin to despise it . . . 'Tis usually cashier'd out of Gentlemen's Houses . . . the *Lingua* will be English'd out of Wales.

That Welsh lived was due to the translation of the Bible into Welsh in 1588 by Bishop William Morgan. In its magnificent language it is the supreme treasure of the *genedl* (nation). Without it, we would have slipped into oblivion as a lost people. Behind this work was sustained and pioneering scholarship into the grammatical structure and lexicography of the Welsh language, and its relationships to other European and classical languages, circulated in books like Gruffydd Roberts's *Dosbarth Byrr ar y rhan gyntaf i ramadeg Cymraeg* ('A short lesson on the first part towards a Welsh grammar') – published in Milan in 1567, one of the earliest printed books in Welsh – and John Davies's famous *Dictionarium Duplex*, of Welsh to Latin, of 1632 (fig. 33).

THE APPROPRIATION OF THE BRITISH PAST

When the country of Wales was annexed, its ancient history was appropriated for the glory of the larger kingdom. The Tudor monarchs made the *Historia* of Geoffrey, and the authority that went with it, almost into an official State doctrine. Wales brought little material wealth to the union, but it could give the immense symbolic wealth to the new Tudor kingdom of a deep and continuous history extending back beyond Caesar to the most ancient city of Troy. The brilliant mathematician and cartographer Dr John Dee from Radnorshire, friend of Mercator and of Ortelius, foreshadowed in his *Perfect arte of navigation* of 1577, the announcement of the discoveries of the Americas by Madoc, a British person within the general ancestral heritage of Elizabeth, that 'red-headed Welsh harridan', and clearly pre-dating any Hispanic claim through Columbus.

It was about this time that the words 'Britain' and 'British' changed their meaning. They ceased to refer exclusively to the inhabitants of the Welsh, Cornish and Breton peninsulae, and were made names for the new Elizabethan England in the broadest context of the islands we now call 'the British Isles'. William Camden called his great topographic history of 1586 *Britannia*, but the Welsh counties and their antiquities form a modest adjunct to its main bulk, which deals with England.

The distinguished, and self-professed English, archaeologist Stuart Piggott sees no irony in summarizing Camden's achievement as having 'set down the historical links that bound the topography of his England to the medieval world, the Saxon past, and to Rome itself'. After the union with Scotland in 1707, audiences sang, 'Britons never, never, never, shall be slaves' in *Rule Britannia!*, but they were not thinking of an Emrys, or Urien or even Owain Glyndwr. Theirs was a Great England, that swallowed up the entire past of these islands into a single history, to be balanced against the foreigners on the European mainland.

So it was that Tudor England created a myth – parts of which are still with us – that all the inhabitants of England, of Wales and later of the rest of the British Isles, were one people with a common ancestry and a shared history. Removed were the invasions, the dispossessions, the fact of some peoples having antecedal origins. The history of 'Great Britain', as in Speed's 1611 book of that title, was represented as a layered cake; the Britons were succeeded by the Romans, by the Saxons and the Danes, by the Normans. All the contemporary descendants shared equally the inheritance of this common history.

This was the ideology of the new and dominant nation of Great Britain.

SAVAGES AND DRUIDS ENTER THE STAGE

Into this historical broth, two other pungent ingredients were to be added, 'savages' from the New World and reconstituted druids of classical memory.

The expanding frontiers of Europe, especially in the Americas, brought accounts of peoples whose customs and technologies were quite unheard of. The most enigmatic were those we now call 'hunters-and-gatherers', people, often naked, who wandered the land in search of game, subsisting on wild animals and grubbing for roots and other plants. They seemed so lacking in culture that they resembled wild beasts. Here were human beings, often beautifully formed physically, who seemed child-like, lacking the moral precepts of adulthood – '*sans roi, sans loi, sans foi*' – 'without king, without law, without faith'.

Shakespeare's Caliban (a word-play on cannibal) was a humanoid creature 'on whose nature, nurture can never stick', a caricature for the amusement of the plebs of the Globe Theatre; but the serious philosophical discourses of Hobbes,

Montaigne and Grotius on the legal rights and moral systems of these less-than-adult people is a major theme of seventeenth-century social and political thought. Biblical analogies invoked the Garden of Eden and Fall of man, and also Esau, 'a cunning hunter, and a man of the field' (Gen. 25, 27). Classical sources provided models, especially from the works of Herodotus and of Lucretius whose first men

> were far tougher than the men of today, as became the offspring of tough earth.
> ... Through many decades of the sun's cyclic course they lived out their lives in
> the fashion of wild beasts roaming at large.

The contemporary 'savage' peoples of America, southern Africa, Lapland, Siberia and a still dimly perceived New Holland began to be seen as living relics from an earlier state of mankind, a stage from which the civilized parts of Europe had progressed. Analogies drawn with such ethnographies began to give meaning to the monuments of Europe, as it began to be realized that they might date from a period far beyond that of the Romans.

As systematic catalogues of archaeological sites and artefacts were compiled, the need grew to place these within a coherent chronological and cultural framework; simple reference to Classical sources became less satisfactory.

Often the seventeenth-century and early-eighteenth-century literature refers to artefacts or stone tools, made by contemporary American Indian and other 'savages', that resembled ancient ones found in Europe. In the same way, explicit recourse to American models was made when depicting and thinking about 'ancient Britons' and their society. Looking back through the mists towards the age of ancient Britain, a mysterious time that seemed nearly beyond knowledge, scholars began dimly to perceive the understanding that could be offered by the relics their topographical surveys noticed in the English countryside, the old forts and strongholds fortified with earth banks, the ancient roads and inscriptions, the old stone monuments and, most famously, Stonehenge, as much a source of wonder to that age as it is to us.

For his 1611 book, Speed had engraved four wonderful illustrations, a man and a woman of 'Ancient Britaines' (fig. 34), and a man and a woman of 'More civill Britaines'. The 'Ancient Britaines' derive directly from John White's illustrations of Virginia Indians; additional iconographic elements come from de Bry's illustrations of Florida, published in Frankfurt in 1580–1. Both figures are naked. The man casually holds the severed head of an enemy; the woman is covered with tattoos. The 'More civill Britaines' – those who might have been seen by a Caesar or Agricola – are clothed, the gentleman wielding a metal sword. The lady, who may be a personification of Boadicea, has a foot discretely peeping out of the bottom of her gown, but close inspection reveals that her ankle, under the outer cladding of civilization, is heavily tattooed.

In about 1656 John Aubrey, of a gentry family in Wiltshire, and descended

34 'Ancient Britaines', as imagined by Speed, 1611, after the model of Virginia and Florida Indians.

from illustrious ancestors in Wales, wrote a delightful reverie on 'The olden time'. He tried to image 'what kind of a countrie this was in the time of the ancient Britons', when the countryside would have been shady dismal woods, 'the inhabitants almost as savage as the beasts. . . . The language British, which for the honour of it was in those dayes spoken from the Orcades to Italie and Spain.' For water craft, they had coracles, like those still used by the poor people of Wales in Aubrey's day.

THE RISE OF DRUIDS AND STONEHENGE

Aubrey's consideration of Ancient British religion brought in another element: 'Their priests were Druids. Some of their temples I pretend to have restored, as Avebury, Stonehenge etc, as also British sepulchres.'

The rise of the druids from minor actors in the Classical accounts of Gaulish society to the dominant paradigm for the pre-Roman past of Britain was part of the romantic renewal of interest in the past that was stimulated both by a wider knowledge of the Classics and by the enigma of the monuments themselves. The stone circles were first connected to the Druids by Aubrey, who reasonably linked the stone temples of the ancient Britons to the people he knew to have been the ancient British priests.

The idea that Stonehenge was a 'British' monument followed Geoffrey and such seventeenth-century sources as John Gibbons in 1666, who saw it as 'an old British Triumphal Tropical Temple'.

After considering the field evidence of the stone circles, Aubrey concluded that 'these monuments were pagan temples which was not made out before'; and, he could decide, these monuments 'were temples of the priests of the most eminent order, viz Druids, and it is strongly to be presumed that Avebury, Stonehenge etc. are as ancient as those times'.

DRUDION AND DERWYDDON, OAK GLADES AND DRUIDS

At this turning-point in the history of ideas about megalithic structures, recourse was made to the Welsh language and to Welsh place-names.

Cerrig-y-Drudion is a mountainous parish in north-west Denbighshire, abutting on to Meirionydd, whose name appears in Camden's original *Britannia* as 'Kerig y Drudion or Druid-stones'; and at Voelas there are some small pillars, 'inscribed with strange letters, which some suspect to be the characters used by the *Druids*'. Aubrey took the matter up in *Monumenta*, writing, 'The hinge of this discourse depends on Mr Camden's Kerrig y Druidd.' Edward Lhuyd (1660–1709), the pioneering palaeontologist, linguist and antiquarian, had decided that Camden's derivation,

> from *Druids*, seems highly probable, tho' not altogether unquestionable: for that the word *Druidion* signifies *Druids*, is, for what I can learn, only presumed from its affinity with the Latin *Druidae*; and because we know not any other signification for it.

'Drud', the supposed Welsh word for 'Druid', was actually a simple borrowing or imitation from the English, first recorded in 1593. It is quite likely that the original derivation was from Camden's account itself! The real meaning of the word 'drud' in the place-name is 'a wild fighter', 'desperate, daring or reckless man'; the word was commonly used to describe furious warfare in the old *Bruts* and should have been known to Lhuyd. So the place-name Cerrig-y-Drudion means the 'stones of warriors or heroes'. It actually has no druidical connection whatsoever.

A second mistranslation involved *derwydd* (plural *derwyddon*), the word which has come to mean 'druid' in Welsh. Its etymology, according to modern linguistic research, may be via the old Breton *darguid* from a proto-Brythonic root *do-are-uid*, whose cognate meanings are lost. Encouraged by Pliny's association of oak trees and druids, John Davies linked this word in his *Dictionarium Duplex* with the Welsh for an oak tree, *derwydden* (plural *derw* or *derwydd*). Lhuyd endorsed the derivation of *derwydd* from *druidae*, and added his own linguistic glosses.

These linguistic by-ways of seventeenth-century philology had profound influence. It is a general belief amongst educated Welsh-speakers today that the word *derwydd* is genuinely old and connected with the oak groves of the ancients.

In seeking insight into Welsh words related to druids, seventeenth-century scholars made an implicit recognition that this language carried within its deep structure a memory of events in Britain older than Anglo-Saxon or even Latin.

Henry Rowlands, Vicar of Llanidan in Sir Fn (Anglesey), stated in his influential *Mona Antiqua Restaurata* (1723), 'the British language is, in its radical parts at least, plainly aboriginal'. Rowlands, adventuring 'through some of the darkest tracks of time, to calculate the Archaeology, and to fetch out and put together some rude strokes and lineaments of the Antiquities of the Isle of Anglesey', pressed further the druidical theory of megalithic monuments. He believed that *derwyddon* took, as their altar, the prone cap-stone of a *cromlech*. New meaning was found in the prefix *crom*, 'bow-backed', in which the bowed was taken to refer not just to the stone, but to the posture of supplicants at prayer. Rowlands concluded that the 'mounts, pillars, heaps, and altars' being the 'monuments of Druidism, peculiarly adapted to the particular rites and ceremonies of their religion and worship, will I think by very few be denied'. His book published, as a full page plate of '*The Chief Druid*', an illustration from Aylett Sammes' *Britannia Antiqua Illustrata* of 1676 (fig. 45): the bare-footed, bearded sage, dressed in a rough cape, holds a hewn wooden staff in one hand, a book of ancient knowledge and a sprig of oak in the other. Are there here also cadences of Prospero:

> Ye elves of hills, brooks, standing lakes, and groves. . .
> I'll break my staff,
> Bury it certain fathoms in the earth,
> And deeper than did ever plummet sound
> I'll drown my book

The Ancient Briton has been promoted from the Caliban of the seventeenth century.

In England, at much the same time, William Stukeley was carrying out detailed field surveys of Stonehenge and other monuments. Some years later, he assembled his manuscripts under the title, *The history of the religion and temples of the Druids*. Having taken Holy Orders, Stukeley attempted to redeem the Druids from their paganism, and made them practise the 'patriarchal religion of Abraham', of which Christianity was but a later version.

From then on, religious and druidic sages were inextricably linked with

35 Image of the Cymric Druid-sage, with staff, beard, book and oaken bough: 'The Chief Druid' of Aylett Sammes's *Britannia Antiqua Illustrata* (1676).

Stonehenge and other megalithic monuments. By the beginning of the nineteenth century, Richard Fenton (1747–1821), a man very much of the new rationalist, industrial age and deeply interested in agricultural improvements and mining techniques, could without a blush describe my own eponymous monument at Ynys-y-Maengwyn as that 'Druidical relick called Cromlech'.

THE INVENTION OF THE 'CELTS'

The word 'Celt' and the idea of the 'Celtic peoples' are so pervasive today, that one assumes that this has always been the case. Yet this was not so, for it was out of these enquiries into linguistic relationships that the concept of Celts developed – whole nations emerging from an academic hypothesis.

The Welsh Enlightenment was marked by a concerted and passionate effort to re-discover the past. I use the word 're-discover' because it was felt that knowledge of the past had been lost with oral tradition in the collapse of independent Welsh society. Welsh scholars of the eighteenth century saw no distinction between studies of the old literary texts, works of language and folklore, and the field investigation of prehistoric monuments and artefacts (figs. 36, 37). Many of the key workers did all of these things, and natural history besides. The Welsh, following a unified theory of their own history, were almost unanimous in thinking that the makers of the megalithic *cromlechau* had spoken a language directly antecedent to their own, that the druids were the same as the bards (*beirdd*); and that the wisdom and cultural traditions of the bards had been

36 Druid of the fantastical kind at the Bachwen cromlech, near Caernarfon: the elderly bard–druid has his hands in supplication before the chambered monument, a healthy oak tree strategically located near by. Watercolour by Moses Griffiths, about 1780.
Courtesy of the National Museum of Wales.

37 'The Bard', illustrating Thomas Gray's (fictitious) account of Edward I's causing all the Welsh bards to be killed after his conquest of Wales in 1282. Oil by Thomas Jones, 1774.
Courtesy of the National Museum of Wales.

transmitted directly, through the poets and bards, to the present. By the end of the eighteenth century, the correlation of bard, druid, *cromlech* and the Welsh language had taken deep roots as the enthusiastic Celto-mania beautifully parodied by Thomas Love Peacock in his *Crotchet Castle*.

PRIMROSE HILL, LONDON, 1792, AND THE GORSEDD Y BEIRDD

At the autumnal equinox, 22 September 1792, there occurred a strange ceremony at Primrose Hill in north London. Four Welshmen, claiming to be Bards of an ancient and secret order descended directly from the Druids, announced they would divulge Druidical secret knowledge for the first time in the English language. According to the *Morning Chronicle* of 26 September, 'The wonted ceremonies were observed. A circle of stones formed, in the middle of which was the *Maen Gorsedd* (throne stone), or altar, on which a naked sword being placed, all the Bards assisted to sheath it', because the '*Bards of the Island of Britain*, for such is their ancient title, were the heralds and ministers of peace'. (Notice the resemblance of the Primrose Hill circle to Stonehenge, which has a flat slab, the 'Altar stone', at the centre of its circle.) The Bards appeared in insignia of three separate orders. During the ceremony 'Bardic Traditions' were recited, and several odes. An ode to Liberty castigated British involvement in the African slave trade:

Join here thy Bards with mournful note,
They weep for Afric's injur'd race,
Long has thy Muse, in worlds remote,
Sung loud of Britain's foul disgrace.

The *Chronicle* explained:

Druidism which the Welch rightly calls *Bardism*, has been sought for in vain by historians, in Greek, Roman and other foreign authors. They are now informed, if they will attend to it, that any regular Welch Bard can in a few minutes give them a much better account of it than all the books in the world; and at the same time the most convincing proofs, that it is now exactly the same that it was two thousand years ago.

Thus, it was said, the English language was first used in the ceremonies; it had been 'opened (as we phrase it), and proclaimed a Bardic language, to be used in future, for ever, as well as the *Ancient British*, or *Welch*, by the Bards of the Island of Britain'. A meeting was announced for the following year, when an Ode in the English language would tell of 'Rhitta Gawr – Rhitta the Giant', a famous Chief of the Ancient Britons, who exterminated so many despots that he made a robe of their beards. Among the bards who revealed these secrets were William Owen, author of the Welsh grammar, David Samwell, Captain Cook's surgeon on his last voyage, and Edward Williams, universally known by his 'bardic' name Iolo Morganwg, the 'rogue elephant' of Welsh literature. Iolo became so obsessed with Welsh history and literature that he went beyond literary scholarship to create or forge an entire literary corpus regarded, for the best part of a century, as amongst the greatest triumphs of medieval and early Welsh poetry. His forgeries are so well executed that it took a major act of scholarship this century to separate the genuine from Iolo.

To dismiss Iolo as merely a forger is to miss the point. Iolo was a man of two worlds, living at a time and in a place where Welsh rural life and the Welsh language was being swamped by industrialization and massive immigration. His other passion was the defence of the country speech and idiomatic dialect of his own people of Glamorgan, despised by the linguistic aristocrats of Gwynedd as 'Gibberish, Hottentotice'.

At the Caerfyrddin (Carmarthen) Eisteddfod of 1819, Iolo held a Gorsedd within a few hundred yards of the relic of Merlin's shattered oak tree and made a ring of stones from pebbles in his pocket. He claimed that the secret lore of the Bards went back in unbroken tradition, beyond Caerwys and the Lord Rhys's celebrated Eisteddfod at Aberteifi in 1176, into the oak groves and standing stones

38 Druidical recruiting poster, signed by Lloyd George.

of the distant past The modern poets, the *beirdd* of the old books, the druids of prehistory – all carried the same torch.

THE DRUID–BARD AS NATIONAL SYMBOL

Since the National Eisteddfod of Wales was founded in 1860, the Gorsedd has been integral to the institution. As the century progressed, the ceremonial paraphernalia and the dress of the bards and Gorsedd officials were elaborated. They were re-designed by Hubert von Herkomer and the sculptor Goscombe John at the end of the century, on the model of Meyrick and Smith's *The costume of the original inhabitants of the British islands* of 1815. The Arch-druid wears a gorget of gold taken directly from the Celtic Iron Age hoards of Hallstatt or Llyn Cerrig Bach, and the crown has a metal filigree-worked chaplet of oak leaves, capped by Iolo Morganwg's three-lined arrow-like cryptic emblem – the logo of his druidism.

The bard as Druid has become the very essence of Welsh identity. During the First World War, our patriarch abandoned the pacifist precepts of Iolo and appeared on a recruiting poster, harp in hand and cromlech in the background, his finger calling the Welsh nation to arms against the oppressor (fig. 38). The picture was the frontispiece for the book produced by the 'National Fund for

39 Ceremonial in the new stone circle at a modern *Eisteddfod*. The author is admitted into the Gorsedd, 1983.

Welsh Troops to provide additional comforts for Welsh regiments at home and abroad', and it was personally recommended by David Lloyd George 'to all Welsh people throughout the world'. Interestingly, the book is an anthology of poetry and song, including extracts from the *cynferidd* and Geoffrey of Monmouth. Does every nation send its sons to battle with the hymns of ancient poets in their inner ears?

The modern Eisteddfod has reached the television age, and the Bards and their ceremonies have adapted accordingly (fig. 39). For the 'National', held in a different town each year, a large stone circle is built according to Iolo's plans, themselves evocative of Stonehenge. In the centre of a circle of upright stones is the Maen Llog (Logan Stone), a flat rock on which the Archdruid and other senior officials receive and robe new members and sometimes deliver homilies on the aims of the Gorsedd. Three Orders wear robes of green, of blue, and of white (fig. 40). Entry into the first two is usually by examination in Welsh literature or music. The Green Robe is offered for various services to Wales, in the past mostly to businessmen and aldermanic dignitaries; recently, and to much public acclaim, Rugby Union footballers and jockeys have been included. David Samwell would have approved.

The two main competitive events of the Eisteddfod are for poetry, strict metre and open metre. Under television lights, the bards of the Gorsedd walk down the aisles of the huge pavilion, packed by about 6,000 people. The Archdruid is a famed poet and a literary leader of the nation. The horns are blown, the great sword half unsheathed with the challenge, 'Is there peace?', to which the assembled throng answers, 'Peace,' and the sword re-sheathed. The prayer of the Gorsedd is sung. When his *nom de plume* is announced by the judges, the winning poet identifies himself, by standing up in the auditorium (usually at the back!). There is a wave of excitement and acclaim as he is recognized and led on-stage. Symbolically, this recognizes the pivotal role of the poet and scholar in Welsh culture: it is they who have kept the song – and the society – alive.

Ceremonials reflect the needs of a people. In Wales, 'a land so devoid of pageantry', the Gorsedd, the standing stones, the weave of antiquarian fantasy, the deep historical resonances, provide 'that element of drama, colour and symbolism for which most Welsh people yearn, and to which they so eagerly respond'.

THE LAND CLAIM OF THE WELSH DISPOSSESSED

I could say: 'This is my land claim, and it is good.'

We, the Cymry are the true Britons, the inhabitants of this island from earliest times. The story I have told is a story of dispossession. First they took our land, and our old monuments on it – the temples and burial-places of our ancient British forefathers. No temple is grander, no temple better shows the grandeur of

40 HM the Queen in bardic dress, as a young woman in the 1950s: 'Ei Mawrhydi y Frenhines yng Ngwisg Gorsedd y Beirdd fel "Elisabeth o Windsor"'.

that British age, than Stonehenge, greatest of the ancient stone circles of Britain. There are megalithic monuments over most of western Europe, but that particular form, the setting of standing stones arranged in a circle or ring, is peculiar to the British Isles. It is the stone circle, of all ancient monuments, that is specially of our making.

As they took our land, so did they take our history. The names of Britain the land and of the Britons the people were taken away from us, and given instead to some alien hotchpotch of *nouveaux arrivistes*, whose land this was not – until they took it from us. The history of the Britons was reduced to the history of the Welsh, an eccentric, marginal adjunct to the invented 'real' history of England and of Great Britain, whose allegiance they stole. The history of the Welsh itself was left to rot, while the Welsh were distracted by the soft comforts of the English court.

When, at last, we understood our deception, it was nearly too late. Where was our history? Where was our past? It was forgotten, burnt, neglected beyond recovery. We clung instead to accidents in place-names and mistakes in their interpretation. Iolo could not revive the knowledge of Welsh history, for Welsh history had been lost. Instead, he re-made a history; he created a 'timeless ancient ritual' of Gorsedd which is not a timeless ancient ritual at all, but a thing of our own times that has been made by us in the manner we wish.

And yet these things have a truth. There *was* an ancient British past, and its strengths and sinews are the spirits that live in the Welsh culture today. In this way we, the dispossessed, have recovered our history, and the new history that we have restored and re-made has become real.

The name and the land are still lost to us. We are called Welsh when we are Britons. The greatest of our ancient places, the stone ring that foreigners named Stonehenge in their foreign tongue, is denied to us. The legal owner of Stonehenge today is a thing that calls itself 'English Heritage' – but we know that Stonehenge is not a Saxon matter, and it has no place in any proper conception of an *English* heritage. The people in whose care has been placed 'Côr y Cewri' – the 'Court of the Giants', the 'Court of *our* Giants' – call themselves English, and think themselves to be British in a wrong and new sense.

This would be my land claim to Stonehenge, as the sacred place of my forebears.

AFTERWORD: FROM STONEHENGE TO TASMANIA

The land claim set out here is a partial thing – as all land claims must be that seek an exclusive control, a narrow possession by whichever group has the better 'legal' claim. As a Welshman myself, I feel a loss that my country has suffered, in its marginal place on the edge of a dominant England. In Wales we speak English, for the most part. Our culture has to withstand the onslaught of English-language words and English-language ideas. Much of our country is owned by outsiders.

In my profession of archaeology, I study for the most part the early human settlement and occupation of Australia – a land that has been lost to outsiders by its indigenous people and traditional owners. Some native peoples of Australia survive, as the Welsh do, but they are marginal survivals in a land directed by others.

In particular I have worked in Tasmania, the island where the confrontation between the native and the in-comer was the nastiest and most complete; the native peoples of Tasmania and their cultures were not just pushed to the margin, but almost exterminated by the newcomers. Today the politics of ethnic identity in Tasmania seeks to assert an exclusive ownership over all the archaeological remains, extending back to the last Ice Age.

It is this experience, above all, that leads me not to pursue the land-claim that I have set out here. It is the partial pursuit of property rights – the claim *by* one group or *by* one culture that is necessarily placed *against* other claims – that is the source of narrow sectarianism. Stonehenge does not 'belong' to the Welsh, or to any one else. Rather, it is a thing to be known and held in common by all who regard it. Like the Ice Age occupation caves of the Tasmanian Pleistocene, it forms part of the common heritage of mankind.

In 1606, at the height of ferment over the island's national identities, much the same view was taken by the Renaissance epigrammist John Owen of Plasdu, Llanarmon, a former pupil of William Camden at Winchester:

Tecum participant in nomine Scotus et Anglus;
Iam tu non solus, Walle, Britannus eris.

By name, Scots and English are with thee;
Now Welshman, not alone, shall thou British be.

CHAPTER FOUR

TRIAD //\: THE DRUID KNOWLEDGE OF STONEHENGE

Tim Sebastian

I went to the Garden of Love
And saw what I never had seen:
A Chapel was built in the midst
Where I used to play in the green.

And the gates of this Chapel were shut,
And Thou shalt not writ over the door;
So I turned to the Garden of Love
That so many sweet flowers bore.

And I saw it was filled with graves
And tombstones where flowers should be;
And priests in black gowns were walking their rounds
And binding with briars my joys and desires.

WILLIAM BLAKE

PROLOGUE

Many claims have been made as to who built Stonehenge ever since people began puzzling over its use and purpose – from Atlanteans to giants, from Phoenicians to Vikings. My own personal viewpoint is that it was, and is still, a Temple, or rather *the* Temple of the nation. Not a ruin, or monument of lost traditions, but a living Temple still in use (fig. 41). For me the question posed by this book, 'Who owns Stonehenge?', is easily answered: the nation owns it.

Another, more important question is, 'Who should be allowed access to Stonehenge, and on what grounds?' It is this question that I address in this 'Triad for the New Age'. I would like you, the reader, to consider the three circles of Stonehenge, the circles of past, present and future, how they overlap and interlink, giving a ground-plan of the spirit of the place, and therefore a guide to how the matter of Stonehenge may be solved.

AN ARCHAEOLOGICAL DILEMMA

The evidence produced by the adept archaeologist supplements what little we know of those deceased generations; as Julian Richards of the Trust for Wessex Archaeology has said, 'I feel that archaeology cannot answer all the questions posed by Stonehenge.' Archaeologists may hope to find only an evidence of the past, as artifacts and token samples; that these provide an idea of what may have happened in the past I do not deny but they are unequivocally dead, devoid of thoughts and personalities, devoid of speech. We gain virtually no idea of what they meant to their real owners, or of the thoughts and attitudes of those now lifeless folk. This caused me anxiety as a private archaeological student and as a practising amateur archaeologist. I now feel that I may be able to shed light into the void between archaeological theory and mystical conjecture. Instead of merely finding evidence and constructing theories, why not find, if you can, the cause of the development of mankind, the root of every man's existence? The spirit of the nation. The sacred landscape around the ancient sites was in part formed by the footprints of our ancestors, who walked and danced at the seasonal celebrations, from the ancient past right up until the Second World War (fig. 42). To say that we somehow damage the landscape today by following these traditions is absurd and blatant rubbish, especially whilst foreign tourists, who have no special interest, are allowed excessive right of access.

41 A circle of Life around our Temple.
Photograph by Alan Lodge.

Will · Will · have · Wilt · tho · Will · Woe · Win ·

42 The Secular Order of Druids is one of the modern orders that carries the old Druidic tradition (above). Druidic imagery reflects the spirit of its inspiration as on the front cover of the new Druidic magazine (opposite).

THE HIDDEN TREASURE

Life is a mysterious adventure. We are invited in. We must walk humbly because the mystery is beyond us. It leaves its signs for all to see. They tell of a power that is greater than the material from which they are made. Once upon a time when the world was wrapped around by a snake biting its own tail, the Wise Men were Seers; men whose vision extended beyond mere sense impressions.

In England we can view the long barrows and the henges, the Roman villas and temples, the medieval cathedrals and renaissance palaces, the factories and power stations of recent times. Much has disappeared but the traces remain. The imprint remains in the culture like a lost secret. Many peoples have given England her identity: prehistoric peoples, Celts, Romans, Anglo Saxons, Danes and Normans and a multitude of immigrants. Spiritual wisdom has come in many guises; each people had its gods. The chief God of one dispensation would become the shadowed exile of the next. Elements intermingled, were assimilated and entangled. Customs and folklore carried what the dominant culture of the time could not reject. Christianity became the dominant religion but assimilated much that it found, and there were different traditions within Christianity. The fate of western civilization, however, was the path of budding rationality, by which we have reached incredible heights of clarity and precision in science and technology. To gain these sharp definitions, we cast out the twilight world with its dreamy-eyed focus. The Greek philosophers began the procedure of separation which reached its climax with Descartes' 'I think, therefore I am', a statement that drew a sharp line between spirit and matter.

The Enlightenment finished the job by declaring everything not within the bounds of reason to be backward superstition or sentimentalities. Because man

really does not exist without his natural richness of dreams and visions these were forced underground. During the Middle Ages, in the secret recesses of the Kabbalists' studies, the Troubadours' love poetry and the Alchemists' laboratories, the world of the psyche flourished to a degree we are only beginning to appreciate.

We could all be losers if we are not concerned for the soul of the nation, if we do not understand our inheritance and our identity. Already much has been lost including the habit of celebration, which religion and custom brought to us as refreshment when they were alive and well. Perhaps they still are if we turn to them. Imaginal reality, when not underground, was neatly relegated to those people or moods outside the 'normal' stream of life. In the words of Shakespeare, 'The lunatic, the lover and the poet are of imagination all compact.'

CIRCLE 1, THE CIRCLE OF ANNWN . . . THE PAST

'In the beginning God created the world (since no one knows any better, and since this myth is sufficiently vague not to offend any rational person, while satisfying the minds of children, it seems quite suitable for today – provided people do not take it too literally).'

So John Michell started one of his articles of historical revelation. So I start mine; as Mr Michell lends weight to the whole subject, I return and refer to his writings throughout this 'Little history of the matter of Britain, its Druids and their temple'.

The Druidic myths say: 'In a remote time, long, long before anything was known of Celtic invasions or our prehistory, tradition ascribes the first planting of the Druid system by a colony in these isles of Britain.' One up for oral tradition, say I.

So it was that world (Atlantean) civilization survived for 11,000 years, or more, until the first beginnings of the Stonehenge complex. That building – now covered by the illegal car park, where once stood a pine enclosure – represents the first ceremonial use of the summerlands on the Wiltshire plains.

Within an archaeologically short period from the setting-up of this ceremonial centre, the world suffered environmental disasters that obliterated from record this first world culture, through the explosion of the volcano Hekla on Iceland, one of the ceremonial heartlands, in about 9400 BC. This is demonstrated in the untranslated works of the great Russian volcanologist Professor Zhirov.

As the dust settled and British society regained its seasonal ceremonial lands, the Stonehenge landscape again became a focal point for festivities; by 4000 BC there was the beginning of what we call 'Stonehenge Phase 1' and Robin Hood's Ball (whose site has been decimated by the activities of the Royal Artillery and their war machines).

By 3500–3000 BC the aboriginal population, who set up the first farming communities, opened the Durrington flint mines and built the Cursus as a focal point for seasonal games.

At this period, the great sanctuary at Avebury was beginning its life as a religious and ceremonial centre, the timber building on Overton Hill being the balance to the magnificent water temple, made from 3000 oak trees, that straddled the River Kennet. This complex with its stone avenues and earth embankments that join river to circle echo exactly the little-noticed earth embankments that lead to the River Avon from Stonehenge. They are part of an enormous plan to create a landscape of festivity and religious celebration that culminates with the building of the Woodhenge, Durrington Walls and Yarnbury Castle complexes.

THE WINGED HARPERS OF THE WEST

Sometime during this period, 4000 to 1500 BC, the first national government in Britain was set up, a government of Bards who ruled by Orphic methods. As John Michell tells us, 'They disseminated order and harmony in society, through the medium of their music, which was based on the true harmonies and proportions found in nature.' We will see, in the last circle, how John has recodified, or rather revealed, this Bardic system for today's generation.

We must first see how, and why, this first truly national government became atrophied and had to expand, and how the misinterpreted legends of human sacrifice were a part of this Golden Age.

Sometime around 1300 BC, volcanic activity again had its effect, displacing the peoples and causing the Celtic procession across the Middle East, through Europe and into Britain. This little-understood – and archaeologically and politically manipulated part of history – starts with volcanic turmoil and climatic change.

The story of the coming of the Celts starts with the displacement of the aboriginal population of southern Africa. Their great trek, up the east coast of Africa to Ethiopia and beyond, into a land they already knew of, is emblazoned across the walls of caves at Brandenburg, South Africa. To see an image of proto-Celtic culture, one only has to study this panoramic procession, and its 'White Goddess'.

'The sun is darkened, the earth sinks into the sea.' So goes the prophecy of the Sybil, and the Icelandic Saga. In 1150 BC, Hekla on Iceland again erupted with such force that the Scottish Highlands became uninhabitable; at least 600,000 people, the Scottish archaeologist John Barber shows, were displaced into southern England. Take this effect, not only in Scotland, but also in Norway, Sweden, Ireland and possibly parts of Wales, and add the Celtic 'invasion'; this southern English population 'explosion' was enough to flood the Bardic cycle into the need for a more aggressive political system.

The Druidic section of this Bardic system codified and enforced the law in the series of proportions and harmonies used by the Orphic system. The sacred king became a man with political, as well as ceremonial, power. The Bronze Age Sword of Peace became a symbol of rule by execution. It is my belief that many, if not all, so-called human sacrifices are in effect executions for criminal and social disorder; they are no sacrifices to deities. Execution as a rule of law has persisted, even in the most civilized societies, until the present day.

In Stonehenge 4, the final phase at 1000 BC, blue stones from Preseli were set up in a tribal amalgamation between the clan chiefs of England and Wales, cementing Welsh deeds to Wessexian lands.

The same may be true for other ceremonial sites in England, the stones placed at these sites acting as deeds of gift to displaced peoples. The Stone of Scone may be a deed of gift between England and the displaced Scots. There is archaeological evidence that the Stonehenge bluestones were part of an existing stone circle that was moved.

As this new system of ceremonial 'land control' continued over the millennia, many other sacred sites accommodated the expanding population, such as the recently discovered water temple at Flag Fen in the Fenlands of Cambridgeshire, that used four million oak, ash and elder trees to construct (a tree alphabet?) a complex so large, 270 m (900 feet) in length, that its chief investigator states, 'The scale of this complex will come as a shock to the archaeological world. It now looks as if Britain's prehistoric cultures were substantially more advanced politically and socially than we have previously admitted.'

So even 2000 years on this landscape can be seen to conform to the Stonehenge and Avebury patterns. The traditional ceremonial structure of society was intact and developing in its sophistication until that fateful date of 55 BC which heralded Julius Caesar's expedition into these isles.

QUIDAM ADVANAE . . . 'THESE ROMANS ARE CRAZY'

Julius Caesar was soon repulsed, but persisted in his famous propaganda exercise against the native inhabitants of these isles, crude disinformation techniques that have no love of truth. Two other expeditions were abortive, and it was not until AD 43 under Claudius that the Romans finally managed to grab some foothold in Britain.

The Druids of the college of Glastonbury, Llantwit Major (founded by Eurgan, daughter of Caradoc and wife of Salog, Prince of Old Sarum) and Stonehenge were the first to convert to Christ, acknowledging him within the framework of the Druidic system and encouraging the foundation of the Culdich church, the 'church of certain strangers'.

This union of two compatible religious systems was a cause of the great revolt against Roman occupation in AD 47, a revolt so successful that Suetonius Paulinus was given the job of obliterating completely the Druids, Culdees, their families and culture. After dealing with the Druids (many escaped into the Welsh marches), the Romans turned their attention to the other symbol of the old religion, Stonehenge. In AD 62 Vespasian launched an attack on the choir, killing Aeddan Foeddog, son of Kaw (known as Ambrose) and pulling down many stones. That is why Stonehenge is known to this day as 'The choir of Ambrosius'. It was not until the time of Constantine the Great (the first home-grown Emperor) and the council of Arles that the British church gained true acknowledgement; his edict of Milan in AD 313 firmly established a Celtic Christian empire under jurisdiction from Britain.

So things remained until that second terrible date in the religious history of these Isles, the coming of Augustine and his imperial missionaries from the spiritually bankrupt Rome in AD 587. When 1200 Culdich Christians were slaughtered at Bangor in AD 613, Augustine's task was coming to its conclusion, and by AD 664 the Roman church was implanted in these lands. Stonehenge was left alone and unused on the windy plains of Wessex until it became all but unknown.

THE IMMORTAL MAGICIANS

By the year AD 1000 the Grove of Druids, Ovates and Bards, founded by Haymo of Faversham, flourished at Oxford, then the centre of the country. Associated with them were those great mystics who were very strong in the spiritual body called the British or Celtic Christian Church. When William the Conqueror made life difficult the grove became a shadow behind the name of Mount Haemus; its persecution resulted in the 'Baronial Rebellion' of AD 1075. William's successor, Rufus the Red King, re-established Druidic rites at his court until his ritual death in the New Forest, at Stoney Cross, at the autumn equinox of 1100.

Geoffrey of Monmouth's *History of the Kings* spearheaded a Celtic revival. The re-establishment of the Mount Haemus Lodge by Philip Brydydd, the Bard of Siluria, in 1245 secured the Druidic succession. After Henry IV, 'that false and perjured knight', usurped the throne in 1399, Owein Glendwr – the great grandson of Llewellyn, last true Prince of Wales – launched a highly successful revolt against Henry IV. Its success was ascribed to his Druidic knowledge and magical powers, which he used to bring thunderstorms, as well as employing spell-casters to stop the advance of his enemies, the practices Strabo and Tacitus say the Druids used. With Owein we find the continuation of unbroken Druidic traditions. He is the spiritual founder of many witchcraft cults now practising in Britain; the word 'witch' is itself cognate with Druid, coming from the word *wicca* and meaning wise, and the daggers, swords and cauldrons used by witch cults also show their Druidic ancestry. Owein Glendwr, when in London, was responsible for the institution of a Druidic society, at an inn in Pentonville, the

Merlin's Tavern. Its cellars led to a cave in the middle of the hill of Penton, which was crowned with a stone circle. In this cave Merlin was said to live, making astrological observations with a telescope of the type also mentioned in Strabo. These cellars and tunnels were bricked up early in the 1900s, and the Tavern demolished to flatten any traces of these Druidic remains.

By 1515 European Druidic lodges were being established, a process that continued until 1650. At this time the Druidic lodge at Maiden Bradley, called the crafty Druids, was suppressed with a false story of them showing travellers the pickled body of the baby Jesus in a jar; its land was given to John Pope. And, Stukeley informs us, an engraved tablet of tin was found at Stonehenge; he believed it was a memorial of the founders of the monument because the characters were unintelligible to the most learned antiquaries.

The seventeenth century saw the publication of Camden's *Britannia* and a renaissance in Celtic–Druidic revelation that was interrupted by the Duke of Buckingham and King James I. The Duke desecrated the centre of Stonehenge, where many items were dug up and stolen; they included precious metal Druidic ritual ornaments, a golden cape of an Arch Druid and a ritual silver-tipped ram's horn; as well as the original altar stone, which was purloined by James I for desecration ceremonies at St James' Palace, Westminster. It is believed that this altar was broken up after the desecration so it would never be used again by the true faith and old religion. The second action was the commissioning of 'Out-i-goe' Jones' Roman polemic, the most outrageous misinterpretation of Stonehenge. Some of Dee's chosen few still supported and published Druidic lore; most notable of their writings are John Fletcher's play *Boudica*, Michael Drayton's verse *Polyolbion*, Milton's great *Lycidas*, Thomas Smith's *Stigma de Druidism*, and Thomas Hobbes of Malmesbury's *Leviathan* in 1651.

All this activity had its flowering in the works of John Aubrey, especially his *Templa Druidum*. Aubrey's work led the new King Charles II to a great interest in Stonehenge and the Druidic antiquities. Aylett Sammes introduced the popular view of the Druidic costume and staff, and by 1694 John Toland and Aubrey began to reinstate Druidism as an active religion.

THE ORDER OF DRUIDS

In England the new activism started with the foundation of the Kit Kat Club, not Druidic in form, but Druidic in spirit and social intercourse. The most famous date in Druidic history falls a year later, 1716, with the initiation of the Order of Druids by John Toland, William Stukeley and Lord Winchelsea on Primrose Hill, London. The Grand Chapter of the Antients, one of the first publicly acknowledged freemasonry lodges, was announced in 1717.

In 1722 Stukeley set up the Society of Roman Knights; Lord Winchelsea receiving the title of Cingetorix of Avebury, Roger Gale the title of Venutius,

43 Stukeley drawing of ancient Celts about their sacred learning, in a circle and with a Stonehenge beyond.
From the collection of the Bodleian Library, Oxford.

44 The Bath circus, built by Druid John Wood after the model of the plan of Stonehenge.

and Stukeley the title of Chyndonax, named after the Gallic Druid. In this way Stukeley was elected the first Arch Druid of the modern cycle. At the ceremonies of the Society in the year 1724 Mr Thomas Hayward, the then owner of Stonehenge, was declared the first Arch Druid of the Isles, and Druid-o-mania was unleashed on an expectant England – sometimes not with the best of results. General Marshall Conway desecrated the Druidic temple remains in Jersey, which were taken away to England and re-erected in his garden at Henley!

With defilement there came also enlightenment (fig. 43): the great John Wood had visions of his circus of the ancients in Bath (fig. 44), and John Toland published his famous treatise, *History of the Druids*. Juliana Papjoy, the mistress of Beau Nash, set up home in a hollow oak tree, holding court as one of the first lady Druids of the modern cycle. In 1740 Stukeley published his monumental *Stonehenge* and in 1743 his *Abury*; in 1742 John Wood published his Bath circus, based on the plan of Stonehenge, and established the temple of Abaris/Bladud at Bath. In 1771 John Smith's book on Stonehenge, *Choir gaur – the grand orrery of the ancient Druids*, was published, and in 1772 a rocking stone at Rishworth initiated as a Druid site. The Marquis of Queensberry – Freemason and Druid-patron of John Gay, who wrote his *Beggars' Opera* while staying in a cave at Avebury (the cave is still there) – took over ownership of Stonehenge in 1777, the same year as the initiation of a bardic site at Harptree in Somerset. In 1781, Henry Hurle founded the Ancient Order of Druids at the Old Kings Tavern, Poland Street.

GOLDEN YEARS OF THE DRUID RENAISSANCE

These next years were the golden Years of the Druidic Renaissance (fig. 45). Reverend John Ogilvie published his *Fane of the Druids*, encouraging William Godwin, from Wisbeach, Somerset, to throw up his holy office. Hurle founded three lodges in the west country: Number Ten, Mona, at The New Globe Tavern, Christmas Steps, in Bristol; Number Eleven, the Anglesey Lodge; and Number Twelve, Trifingus, at the Seven Dials, Bath. Later the Order of the Twenty Four Elders was solemnized at the Congress of Bards, who assembled at Primrose Hill at the autumnal equinox of 1792. A stone circle was formed; in the middle was the Mayen Gorsedd or altar, on which the naked sword was placed. William Blake became the Arch Druid of the Isle, and began to publish his prophetic books.

The nineteenth century marks the great re-establishment of the Druidic Romantic movement. So rapid is change in our times that it seems as if the

45 Stonehenge as it was seen in the Golden years of the Druidic Renaissance. Watercolour drawing by James Malton, 1800.
Courtesy of the Victoria & Albert Museum.

Romantics were roaming the earth almost as long ago as the dinosaurs! They left a rich inheritance of high challenges, still to be met and mastered. The Romantics wished to secularize all religious and spiritual striving. Religious faith was to be surpassed by the drama of self-discovery: Coleridge coined the term 'self realization' – finding the divine in oneself. Though they expressed it in different and diverse ways, all the Romantics were concentrated on the quest for the Grail. Just because we are over-saturated today with 'paths' to self-realization, we should not be oblivious to a momentous shift: the Romantics sought to relocate the perennial search for God into the realm of human subjectivity *exclusively*! God is then to be found in two ways . . . either in oneself, or through or with another. The first is the self-realization of Coleridge, the second is anticipated in the legend of Tristan and Isolde, where the passionate love between woman and man assumes more power and significance than the love between humanity and God. 'Romance' in this sense supersedes religion because it makes human love into a religious experience, the direct encounter of the divine within human nature itself.

In all this the Druid spirit had its place. A flurry of Druidic site initiations took place in 1820 – at Masham, Yorkshire, and at Wimpole Hall, Cambridge, and in Hyde Park, London. Gaffer Hunt became the Arch Druid of Stonehenge at the sponsorship of Dr John Hill and John Wood. In 1833 a revolt in the Wessex lodges led to the foundation of the 'United Ancient Order of Druids'. By 1834, the Albion Lodge of the Ancient Order was re-founded at Oxford on the remains of the Mount Haemus Lodge. After William Godwin's and William Blake's deaths, the Romantic movement was carried forward by the large circle of artists they had encouraged; the most notable of this 'grand lodge of artists' were Samuel Palmer, Thomas Cole, James Malton, William Marlow and Thomas Jones – who all painted Stonehenge. The year 1840 brought the first British performance of Bellini's Druidic opera *Norma*. At her wedding, Queen Victoria was dressed completely in white with no jewels, just garlanded with flowers – very Druidic indeed. During the 1850s the site of the Agglestone on the Isle of Purbeck was initiated, and Sir Rowland Hill, founder of the Penny Post, initiated a Druids' Cell at Hawksworth, Shropshire. And in 1860 Myfyr Morganwg initiated the rocking-stone and stone circle at Pontypridd, a tradition carried on by Morien, author of *The royal winged son of Stonehenge and Avebury*. The German traditions came together in 1872 with the formation of the 'International World Lodge of Druids'.

At this time, to be precise, a new tradition was founded, to take the Romantic revelations well into the twentieth century. The Theosophical Society was founded by Madam Blavatsky in 1875, the year which saw the birth of the 'beast' Aleister Crowley; the next year saw the birth of that other grand magical master, Gerald Gardiner. The new spirit unleashed by Blavatsky had immediate effect on Druidism; at the Eisteddfod of 1878, the Arch Druid performed a ritual to the Hindu goddess Kali. Even the Christians got in on the act with the foundation of

46 The Arch Druid proclaiming 'the truth against the world', in the gardens of the Inner Temple, London, 1887.

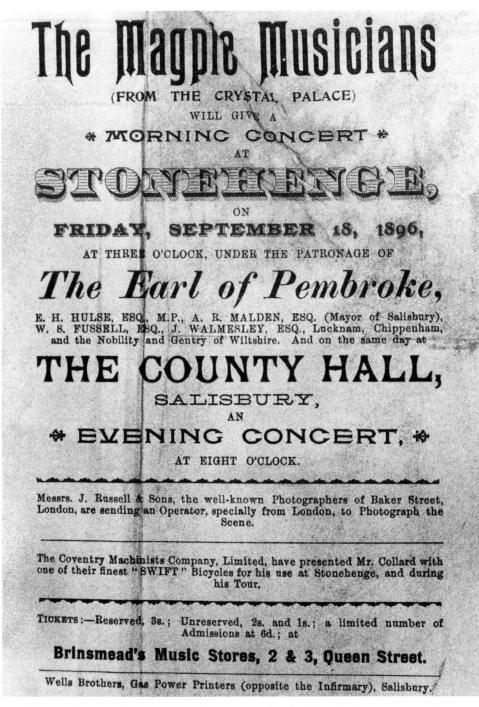

47 Notice of a morning concert at Stonehenge by the Magpie Musicians in 1896.
Courtesy of the Wiltshire Archaeological and Natural History Society, Devizes.

the New Forest Shakers in 1879.

In 1884 Dr Price caused a stir by cremating his son Iesu Crist at Llantrisant, in keeping with Blavatsky's Indian revelations; he was tried at Cardiff Assizes, but acquitted. In 1886 and again in 1887, the Arch Druid, Idris Vychan (Mr Vaughan), Telynor Cymru (The Harpist) and a large congregation proclaimed the first London Eisteddfod in the Temple Gardens, London – a great event that has been suppressed by the authorities; it was echoed in 1986 when the Secular Order of Druids gathered at the spot in commemoration. In 1888 Dr W. R. Woodman, Dr Wynn Westcott and Samuel Liddell MacGregor Mathers founded the Hermetic Order of the Golden Dawn of which the poet W. B. Yeats, Aleister Crowley and Dion Fortune were to become members (indeed, Crowley became its Outer Head).

The close of the old century saw Druidism as a growing force (fig. 46), and Stonehenge as a place of happy resort (fig. 47).

This brings me to an end of the first cycle of Druidic history.

CIRCLE 2: THE CIRCLE OF ABRED . . . THE PRESENT

The twentieth century started with a Druidic fanfare, the publication of Elgar's opera *Caractacus*. In 1900 Lady Poore of Amesbury – the first Arch Druidess of the Isles – had founded her own Druidic order in one of the first acts of the feminist revolution; her group started holding their ceremonies on Normanton Downs. Other initiates in this order are believed to have been the sisters Ella and Dora Noyes, who published their own books on Salisbury Plain.

But soon the divine music was attacked: in 1901 Sir Edmund Antrobus, the proprietor of Stonehenge, erected a fence and started to charge admission to the Temple. Lord Avebury objected strenuously and resigned from the Stonehenge Advisory Committee, saying that it was not sufficiently insistent on the rights of access to the public. For years he had argued the truth, that Stonehenge was held in trust for the nation as a whole. Sir Edmund threatened to sell Stonehenge to America, and Amesbury Parish Council asserted the tradition of free access to the downland for local people. Even the National Trust led a group insisting on a public right of access, a stand it has lamentably reneged on. Mr Justice Farwell found in favour of Antrobus's capitalistic methods, even though that fine and notable archaeologist, Flinders Petrie, had appealed to stop the fences going up. The despoiling of the Stonehenge landscape had begun.

All during this period the Church of the Universal Bond had been celebrating rituals at the Temple. At the 1901 solstice Sir Edmund had the police eject the Druids; Mr C. A. Lardner, the Chief Druid, publicly and ritually cursed Sir Edmund. Five different orders of Druids performed their rites at the Temple during this period, on separate days. In 1904 confrontation with Antrobus erupted again, when the Druids were disturbed while burying the ashes of a

48 Druids at Stonehenge wearing the Indian manner of robes, 1920s.
Photograph from the collection of the Wiltshire County Library & Museum Service.

former Arch Druid in the Temple, as they always had done. They challenged Sir Edmund to have them arrested, but this time he let the ritual continue.

In the war years the Order of Hermetists Druids kept the solstice alive whilst the Golden Dawn kept their vigils at Glastonbury, until Bligh Bond established the Brotherhood of Watchers and 'the Company of Avalon' at Arthur's Shrine.

At the summer solstice of 1914, Chief Druid Dr G. M. MacGregor Reid had not proceeded very far into the rituals before Superintendent Buchanan of the Wiltshire Constabulary called his attention to a notice posted within Stonehenge, illegally prohibiting any religious service within the circle, and told him to desist. When Dr Reid persisted, the Superintendent forcibly ejected him. Dr Reid in true Druidic style, resorted to the time-worn curses against Antrobus. Within a year both Antrobus and his son were dead.

There is a lesson here for all would-be Druids: death curses have to be paid for by the cursors. The pain for this curse swiftly followed. Stonehenge was sold, and the 1913 plan for its transfer to a company of Druids and antiquarians failed. On 21 September Stonehenge was sold to that great local character Cecil Chubb for £6600. Chubb, forever tactful, made peace with the Druids and at least halved the admission charge. Things remained steady for the next few years.

THE GIFT OF THE STONE GRAIL

In 1918, Stonehenge, the Stone Grail, was donated by Chubb to the nation with a strict deed of gift that was later totally broken by the governing authorities. The Druids were asked to legitimize spiritually the handing-over, and it was the Arch Druid who actually handed over the title-deed to national representatives. (All Druidic denigrators should note this action, which alone secures and legitimizes the Druidic claim to Stonehenge as a Temple of the Druids.) Cecil Chubb was knighted for his generosity, by that Welsh wizard Lloyd George, and given honorary membership by the Druid orders. The First World War ended that same year; peace and harmony reigned at Stonehenge for the next 35 years, with a number of Druidic orders celebrating the solstice on different days of the solstice

49 The Herald welcomes the dawn with a fanfare to the four winds at the summer solstice ceremony, 1966, before the Stones were desecrated.
Photograph by Austin Underwood.

period, 20–25 June (fig. 48). During the 1940s, jazz bands regularly played at the solstices at Stonehenge, refuting the modern idea that music is not an acceptable form of entertainment at Stonehenge.

FROM THE UNIVERSAL BOND TO THE BOGLES

By 1955 only the Universal Bond was still celebrating at Stonehenge, the Ancient Order becoming a friendly society. Vaughan Williams, that great collector of English folk song, published his 'Wessex Prelude' or 'Stonehenge Symphony', later the anthem of the Secular Order of Druids. Vaughan Williams, at the end of the 1950s, announced that British music was entering a new phase, completing the first part of the journey towards the New Age.

How true his words turned out to be! The British wave of popular music in the 1960s coincided with the spate of UFO sightings focused on Warminster, on the Stonehenge–Glastonbury ley, which occupied the unique Arthur Shuttlewood throughout this period. 'Mods' came in great numbers to join the solstice celebrations, truly joyful occasions by now, with Morris dancers and Len Buckland's dancing skeleton. All this enjoyment was too much for Professor Atkinson the archaeologist and his moribund crew of anti-Druids and anti-life. The unenlightened approach with which Atkinson met any alternative theory is an indication of a very dull mind indeed.

In 1962 the authorities again erected barriers around Stonehenge (fig. 49). A great debate amongst the Druid brethren ended in yet another split; the Order of Bards, Ovates and Druids gave up Stonehenge and initiated other sites instead, Tower Hill in London and Hunsbury Fort near Northampton. (This group was to include Ken Barlow from *Coronation Street*.)

In 1965 a new and magical order appeared – The Order of the Silver Beetle. Its first act was the materialization at Stonehenge of the Bogles, cut-out wooden figures of young men, one sitting (fig. 50). Their purpose has remained a mystery until this day. I can reveal that they represented the Beatles; the sitting Bogle was a reference to Stewart Best, the drummer who died during their early years. John Lennon was chosen as Bard of this order, its purpose to initiate the New Age through the popular cultural expression of the time, music. The prophecies of the album *Help* now come into sharper focus. The Bardic forces of music at war with other religious orthodoxies are expressed by the 'Fab Four's' battle on Salisbury Plain, around Stonehenge. Other prophecies abound in the history of Beatledom; the Blue Meanies' attack in *Yellow Submarine* is a classic example, a direct prophecy of the Battle of the Beanfield in the heart of the summerlands in 1985. The great Bardic anthem of youth, 'All you need is love', culminated in the album *Abbey Road*, which is rife with reference. Its cover photo is a direct pun on the photo of the Bards and Ovates' first procession at Tower Hill in 1964, Lennon wearing all white and looking all the bit a Druid (because he was) leading the

50 Two of the Bogles, Bob Bogle on the left and Bruce Bogle on the right, who mysteriously appeared at Stonehenge one morning in 1965. Within hours, the custodians took them away and broke them up.
Photograph by Austin Underwood.

other four into the realms of legend. The songs 'Here comes the sun' and 'Sun king' are great Druidic anthems for the New Age; even the older song 'Blackbird singing in the dead of night' echoes the rooks of Stonehenge and its Druidic bird cults. The message is clear to the Silver Beetle generation, 'Boy, you've got to carry that weight a long time, but golden slumbers fill your eyes.' The pure white album will pull you through. Are the white panthers calling to you?

THE FESTIVALS, STONEHENGE, AND THE SEVENTH SON OF THE SEVENTH SON

In 1968 Arthur Shuttlewood saw his first Stonehenge UFO, which 'blacked out entirely before becoming a ring of fire that shot from the stones themselves'. The year 1969 saw the publication of *A View over Atlantis* by John Michell, which reveals the sacred dimensions of Stonehenge as the plan of the new Jerusalem, and gives the New Age motivation and vision.

At the solstice 2000 converts crashed the barbed wire to re-take the centre of the stones for the nation. In 1970 chosen Chief Druid Ross Nicholls and the Order of Bards, Ovates and Druids held a Gorsedd and Eisteddfod on the summit of Glastonbury Tor, at Bealteinne, as Leslie Alcock's excavations at Camelot came to an end and the bronze Arthurian 'A' was revealed to the public for the first time. In Britain, 1970 was the year of festivals; Phun City was followed by the Isle of Wight festival and Lord Montagu's Beaulieu extravaganza. It amazes many people that Lord Montagu – so happy to exploit the people for capitalistic gain – then should be so mean of spirit when he is given the Chairmanship of English Heritage, that he starts to persecute the very generation who had supported his money-making venture years before. Well, that's modern aristocracy for you.

At the Spring Equinox of 1972, the doors to the mysteries were again open, for in that year began a new renaissance of occultism and a new dispensation. In 1973 the seventh son of the seventh son of the sun of Cyprus enters Wiltshire, knocks on the door of St John and is granted admission. He receives a revelation on Copheap and again on Cley Hill.

The Stonehenge free solstice ritual at Warminster, conceived with a group of twelve good Wiltshire men and true, led to the first solstice festival proclaimed in 1974. The sun (the orb not the rag) revealed its splendours; peace and harmony reigned. But in 1975 the Windsor free festival was violently and without warning attacked by the police early one morning. Syd Rawles negotiated with the Queen's Pastor for a withdrawal, and agreement was made that the festival be transferred to Stonehenge. The seventh son was arrested as a subversive, and bound over to The Manor, an infamous psychiatric asylum for the bewildered; there his torment began. The festival went ahead with 200 converts but without their spiritual adviser; some say that the Hawk Lords appeared. I quote from the

51 Our Druidic marriage, at Stonehenge as it should be – but on the tarmac road outside the fence.

Seventh Son's last statement. 'The first dream that I remember is that of myself holding the hand of an older man looking over a beautiful and peaceful valley. Suddenly a fox broke cover followed by hounds and strong horses ridden by red-coated huntsman. The man pointed into the valley and said, "That, my son, is where you are heading." I soon found that out. I am the fox.'

THE SECULAR ORDER OF DRUIDS

The same year, 1975, the Secular Order of Druids was initiated in the presbytery of the parish church at Amesbury, its purposes to spread the Druidic message to the youth of the nation and to act as voluntary guards to the Druidic ritual (fig. 51) in a caring low-key way, to act as a catalyst in bringing together all the Celtic/pagan magical systems of England in a great debate of the future, and to promote the writings of John Michell. 'Secular' implies acting in the present world, a temporal sphere of things, not spiritual or sacred; it also implies a profane order, a lodge of worldly mystics. But we use the term in its meaning of *soeculum*, cognate with *serere* – to sow, by extending a lodge of non-ordained priests over the temporal plain, with the effect of accomplishing a task over a century.

One contributor to this book, after seeing the film of Secular Order activities, exclaimed, 'Well, I never knew Druidism could be so much fun.' I take his point, but it must be said – and as Arch Druid of this Order I must be the one to say it – that our Order is totally unapologetic in our Romanticism. We see our place as conveyors of creative stimuli to the summer solstice. We proudly boast of our Celtic/Christian and Druidic/pagan mixed cosmology. We actively encourage ecumenical debate and dialogues about the spiritual health of our nation. We see the best outlook for this health reflected in the Green and New Age movements. We also, to the best of our ability, discourse with the young on the myths and legends that surround the Temple. We don't mind at all being seen as eccentric, for the secret pages of our whole wonderful cultural tradition and history are bedecked with people, considered eccentric in their time, who were really poets. That said, we are a serious-minded group; it is through the symbols revealed in the myths and legends of this history that the greatest changes in the spiritual health of the nation can be obtained. Our every action is towards this end.

The whole multitude migrated from Windsor to Wessex to join the strange group at Stonehenge known as the 'Wallies of Wessex'. The Hawk Lords revealed themselves to hundreds of eye-witnesses. Later, the Seventh Son, and two of his disciples, were found dead in mysterious circumstances. The prophecy was fulfilled, the blood was spilt. In 1976, the ritual of the Egyptian Book of the Dead was performed at the summer solstice, and many saw visions in the sky. The Seventh Son's ashes were scattered at Stonehenge. In October 1977 glowing lights were seen above the stones, hovering and then changing directions instantly. Compasses went awry, and Army searchlights were deflected by the UFOs, which were caught on film.

By 1978 the Chief Constable of Wiltshire was calling the festival and the Druids nothing more than a bunch of sordid mystics; by the solstice, badges and T-shirts appeared on festival stalls with slogans, 'I am a sordid mystic' and 'Got pissed and mystic', emblazoned on them. Permission was denied for a performance of the opera, *The Henge*. Two thousand records of two tracks from it were given away at Stonehenge at the solstice. Una Woodruff published *Inventorum Natura*, and the House of Lords debated the UFO problem.

The year 1980 was one of the revelation of the teachings of the eight great powers. In 1981 John Lennon, Arch Druid of the Silver Beetle, was shot by the Catcher in the Rye. The year 1982 was one of fertilization, the year of planting, even though; the Freemasons hanged Calvi under Blackfriars Bridge, and the infamous P2 Lodge was established in Britain. The year 1983 was one of fruition, the year of seeking perfection, growth and development – and the year of trust and innocence and being totally open, when people were listening and the teachers were talking to teachers. John Michell published yet another book of revelation, and the first edition of the magazine *Wally* was published at the summer solstice. The *Sunday Mirror* linked Druids, ley-lines and ghosts to various disasters that befell the stars of *Coronation Street*.

The year of the animal, 1984, was the year that balance and harmony between light and dark forces was beginning to achieve a balance. A sort of urgency was spreading amongst the populace. The Wessex-awake group held its first organized rituals at the summer solstice, and Cross published *The history of Wally Hope*, which they gave away with their latest LP. The Freemasons published *Stonehenge revealed* (as a Freemasons' temple), and launched their plans to desecrate the solstice rituals. The last great Hawkwind ritual concert and ceremonial feast took place on solstice evening of this, the last year of the traditional Stonehenge Solstice Festivals.

The following year, 1985, the festival was banned by the government. The advance guard of festival-goers were driven into a field, 10 km (6 miles) distant from Stonehenge, and there the Battle of the Beanfield took place.

That day was the day of the Amesbury Carnival, dedicated to the festival of youth. Other members of the Secular Order and I were at the Carnival when the Battle broke out. Horrified, we went along the public highways to Stonehenge to protest at the violence. When I approached a Police Officer, merely to ask him what could be done, I was immediately arrested. I found myself incarcerated in Amesbury Police Station, in a one-man cell with 16 other people in it. One of these was a young lad of no more than 15 who had had the entire lower part of his jaw dislocated; his whole mouth was just one gaping wound. No matter how much we protested, this young man was not taken to hospital. We were held for three days, and it was only the kindness shown me by officers at Portsmouth Jail that restored any faith in the Police Force.

The next year, 1986, saw the great Tarmac ritual – when the ceremonies had to take place on the main road outside Stonehenge. It also saw Syd Rawles's great rain dance on top of the White Horse in Wiltshire – a rain dance that was to be so successful it didn't stop raining for the next three years. (I'd just like to make a plea at this point for Syd to learn the stopping-of-the-rain dance, which I feel he must have by now.) In this year an incredible amount of leaflets and pamphlets were published on Stonehenge, enough to keep Robin Greenwood's gang – initiated in 1984 at Stonehenge – in recycled envelopes for years. At the great Stonehenge Forum, an amazing event, all the major spiritual bodies came together in Salisbury to debate the Stonehenge issue, and the famous Willie X revealed himself as the messiah to an astonished audience. Syd Rawles was this year accepted as the Seventh Son's true successor. To the Bealteinne gathering, deep in the woods of Wilton, came Christians, pagans, egyptologists, astrologers, Druids, hippies, rainbow warriors, anarchologists, feminists, quakers, Crowleyites, witches, wallies, Kabbalists, and some who were a bit of everything. The aim of this meeting was to try and inform each other of the nature of the various spiritual perspectives in relation to the summer solstice at Stonehenge. This was one of the great spiritual meetings of all time to be seen near the Temple. The same year also saw the great archaeological congress at Southampton which debated the issues; a fragile truce was born from this. The media, when they debated the issues, missed them by a mile.

In this year the Solstice Trust was founded, of which more later. It also saw English Heritage asking certain universities to try and create a tourist-oriented Druidic order, a task they manifestly failed in.

1987

The great trek of the Stonehenge peoples, which began in 1985, was carried on until 1987. I digress here to mention that at the Archaeological Congress of 1986 the authorities unveiled plans for an underground bunker complete with a plastic Stonehenge, a project to try and keep Druids, mystics, hippies, and the poor out of the Temple complex. This plan has been temporarily shelved. By 1987, the by-now-famous 'Order of Medieval Brigands', inaugurated by Douglas Hurd in a television interview, had changed from a trek to a pilgrimage. The Solstice Trust started its campaign for a proper ceremonial site and planned to rebuild Woodhenge. Salisbury Museum put on an Anti-Druid Solstice event to prove that Druids don't exist. The District Council announced their plans to put beacons on Cley Hill, as a homage to war, but refused to pay for it, whilst Druids put up braziers for peace. Accusations of cannibalism were thrown at the solstice ancestors, and BBC2 made a serial out of the Romantic Celtic renaissance.

The summer solstice shone its light on all assembled, and the first true solstice celebration for four years was achieved. The Secular Order and many other orders re-established Glastonbury Tor's ritual triangle, and the Temple of Albion gave the rituals of the Sun to the youth of the nation on solstice morning, live on national television. The Druid order had to fight off the press and the helicopters, but the solstice pilgrims performed the first wheel dance of the New Age, and peace and harmony reigned that day. This same year Mr Fawsi Mitawli, a 53-year-old magnate from Vienna, applied for a million-dollar production of Bellini's *Norma* to be staged at Stonehenge. He was refused. Christopher Chippindale unveiled his Brickhenge in Southampton, during the biggest art show event on Stonehenge ever; within a month reproductions of his work by forgers were being snapped up by art houses for the mere sum of £3000.

The great harmonic convergence took place on 17 August 1987, when the various winged serpent wheels began to turn to dance once again; as they danced, the rainbow lights were seen in dreams all over the world. The year's end saw the initiation of the Order of Olympus at the Greenwich Meridian. Many occult organizations had representatives: the Thelemic Orders of Caliph OTO and Silver Star, the Temple of Olympus representing the Olympian pantheon, various Wicca orders, various Druidic orders, the Hermetic Continuum, and the Temple of Psychic Youth.

CIRCLE 3: THE CIRCLE OF GWYNUYD . . . THE FUTURE – AND THE SOLSTICE TRUST

The matter of Stonehenge is not merely parochial. Whatever happens there is crucially important to the future of this country, and may well determine the shape of things to come and the pattern of a new order on earth.

JOHN MICHELL, *Stonehenge: its history, meaning, festival and future*

On 16 June 1988 a remarkable event occurred in the lecture theatre of the Salisbury Museum, an event that should have an immense impact upon the problems that have surrounded the solstice at Stonehenge: perhaps even upon the very future of the venerable monument itself.

So what was this event that has the power to change the future and bring peace to the present? It was the unveiling of a long-lost oil painting of Stonehenge, by the druid Edgar Barclay (fig. 52), a Victorian artist with an intimate archaeological association with the monument, and a place in the British art scene which is regarded by many as unique.

How can a mere painting, no matter how important artistically, have the power to change the present political climate, and inculcate peace in the minds of the people of the plain? Well, the story behind this painting, its discovery and exhibition is one of remarkable synchronicity and persistent faith in the power of

52 Edgar Barclay's pastoral painting of Stonehenge with the Shepherd of Salisbury Plain.

the henge as a symbol of the eternal city, by a group of courageous visionary and illuminating people, a group who have worked hard over the last four years to bring the solstice celebrations to their proper place in the heartbeat of the British nation. This group is known as the Solstice Trust.

The Solstice Trust was formed in 1986, after the first clashes between the authorities and the solstice celebrants ended in a stalemate that put a stop to the Druidic rituals. This situation has lasted since then, steadily worsening in the violence from both sides. Although the Druids have attempted to show a brave face and muddle through, the ceremonies have been unsatisfactory. So the Solstice Trust has made suggestions, to all sides in the conflict, on how the solstice could be a source of pride and happiness, in a major publication from the Trust, 'The World Garden Site Plan'.

What is the World Garden Site? It is an arena for all, especially designed with the help of artists and environmentalists with an interest in folklore and ritual, as well as advisers from the local, festival and travelling populace. The design of the site and its individual structures have been worked out on the harmonious principles of the New Jerusalem and the secret numerical traditions that lie behind the Garden of Eden mythos. Utmost attention is paid to environmental enhancement and community involvement. The different parts of the site could be connected by paths made of woven wickerwork, like the ancient trackways of Wessex.

Among the Trust's many members and sympathizers are: John Michell, the world-famous author on gematria and sacred sites; David Loxley, the present

Chief Druid of Stonehenge; Janet Cross of the local Quakers, a marvellous example of Christian virtue; Tim Abbott, the slightly eccentric but always amusing town councillor from Wilton; and the famous tipi-dweller and travellers' spokesman Syd Rawles, who has baptized many babies and married many couples over the last 15 years of Solstice gatherings.

The overall site of the Garden would cover approximately 8 ha (20 acres) altogether. It has several elements.

The Stonehenge Musuem

First proposed in the 1920s by the eminent patron of archaeology and innovative genius, Alexander Keiller, the Stonehenge Museum would be a permanent gateway to the whole site. We propose that English Heritage and the National Trust should raise the monies for this part of the project, to house both a library and an artefact display of Stonehenge-related items, plus a gallery for modern and retrospective art exhibitions relating to megaliths: for example, the works of Heywood Sumner, or Keiller's own marvellous photographs.

Woodhenge

An ambitious reconstruction of Woodhenge (fig. 53) could and should be achieved:

1   It would be built by a labour force made up from the many unemployed young

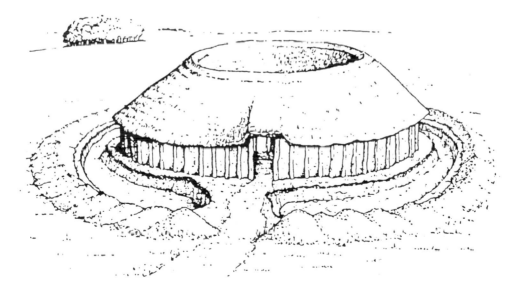

53 The new Woodhenge, from the Solstice Trust's plan for a World Garden near Stonehenge.

115

persons from the local community and festival groups, with help from archaeological and professional advisers – creating employment of an adventurous and stimulating nature.

2   The Woodhenge would be a focal point at solstice time.

3   The remainder of the year, Woodhenge would be a place for artistic and community events, available to the local communities; and it would undoubtedly become a tourist attraction – money raised would go to the Wessex Trust.

The Herbal Clock of the Age

A grand floral design laid out in herbs and medicinal plants, sponsored by herbal and alternative medicine societies, and also a tourist attraction for the summer months, provides space for these interests at the great solstice celebrations.

The Tipi Circle

The world-famous Tipi Circle would be allowed on site at solstice time, as an ethnic centre where racial minority groups from around the world – Hopi, Buddhist, Aboriginal, etc. – would come and promote their cultural inheritance and spiritual views.

The Earthwork

We call this project, perhaps the most exciting and ambitious of the plans that it is our pleasure to put before the reader, an 'Arena for All'.

Apart from its obvious archaeological and scientific potential, we believe this structure will become a popular meeting place for individuals, groups and societies, for it creates great possibilities for theatrical, ritual, communal and scientific uses.

Its building would be sponsored by Earth Mystery groups, who would have responsibility for its management and upkeep. At solstice time it would be used for debates and theatrical performances of an Earth Mystery nature.

The Forest of Charity

The Earthwork could be placed in an already wooded environment, or in an unwooded area with a new forest created around it. The forest would be created by subscription: a person could buy trees, perhaps to commemorate the passing of a loved one, and profits from the sale would go to the charity of the purchaser's choice. The planting of trees by public health authorities and health concern groups, for the victims of meningitis, or AIDS, or other infectious disease, would help these bodies' fund-raising activities whilst forming a public memorial for those who have died. As the forest grew, it would bring home to visitors the number of deaths that infectious diseases claim every year. The beginning of 1990 saw the storms fell many of the Stonehenge trees.

SOLSTICE '88 – THE GREAT DEBATE

Just before the solstice of 1988, English Heritage announced plans to distribute 500 tickets between the 3000 to 4000 people who wished to be part of the event: an unworkable plan that was to lead to discontent and disruption, as the Druid orders said it would. The police helicopter once again was used to completely mar the Druidic ceremony, hanging above the stones, booming out garbled commands. The events of this solstice gathering left not only the Druids but also the nation amazed and dazed at what was really taking place on the sacred plain. Sinister forces were determined, at whatever cost to the people of Wiltshire or to the democratic rights of our nation, to keep solstice celebrations banned into the distant future.

One good thing did emerge from this disturbing scenario; the five major Druid orders after many years began to talk to one another, and also to consider the World Garden Site proposals as one of the only alternatives to the years of conflict that have been foisted upon them. After many meetings throughout the following year these orders debated the problems and solutions to the Stonehenge saga. On 4 June 1989, the day of the Beijing massacre and the death of the Ayatollah, they agreed to form a new Grand Grove of British Druidism to promote the Secular Order's plans for an Eisteddfod in 1990 and the Solstice Trust's World Garden Site.

At the solstice of 1989, banned again from their Temple, these orders met together on Primrose Hill in the capital and re-performed the first Gorsedd ritual of Edward Williams, from 200 years earlier, with a new circle constructed from stones sent by Druid groves from all over Britain. They spiritually connected with many other groups performing rituals at other sites from Devon to Cumbria.

John Michell was duly elected Bard of the Eternal City and Grand Druid Council. The orders unveiled a petition to HM The Queen requesting permission to be allowed to hold the Eisteddfod in 1990 and inviting all to compete for prizes – a Bardic Chair for poetry, Golden Harps for music and theatre, the Golden Bough for healing and Prism of Light for astro-archaeology and film. They processed to Buckingham Palace where they presented the petition – upstaged by 5000 tourists, 57 policemen and the Coldstream Guards. This day will, in the future, be seen as one of the major events of Druidry this century. After the ceremony a member of this gathering flew off to the United Nations 'University for Peace' conference to tell of this event and how it represents a possible source of spiritual and artistic inspiration for the Green movement worldwide.

So what of the future? The first all-England Eisteddfod will be held in 1990 despite the best efforts of the politically isolated group of anti-solsticites. And what other signs of change are there? Well, the European elections held over the solstice of 1989 mark a new chapter in the history of not only our sacred Isle but the whole of Europe, for the gradual adoption of environmental consciousness is the only way forward for our world.

COMING FULL CIRCLE

Within days of the solstice ritual of 1989, mysterious marks began appearing in the cornfields of the Stonehenge landscape, as they have for several years, in single or grouped circles; this time the rings were set in groups the shape of a perfect cross. A new design for a new age perhaps, or something much older trying to tell us something?

Exciting stuff indeed! But isn't there something more tangible on offer for the future? Consider this. . . . During the heatwave of the summer of 1989 (a rare enough event), air-reconnaissance photographs revealed images of 300 unknown archaeological sites, revealing much more of our prehistoric ceremonial past, including new henges in Essex and, most importantly for the Stonehenge story, Welshpool.

A more direct message has been sent to the future by John Michell's *Dimensions of Paradise*. On its cover, a watercolour by John shows the Tree of Life set between the Druidic choirs of Stonehenge and Glastonbury, and at the foot of the tree are emblazoned the words, 'The leaves of the tree were for the healing of all Nations'. When we search amongst the knowledge of John's tree, we find the most important of leaves as far as the Stonehenge problem and its future healing is concerned: his understanding of the placing of Stonehenge at one of the four corners of a ten-sided figure, the centrepoint of which proves to be a spot called Whiteleafed Oak – the meeting point between the three counties, Hereford, Worcester and Gloucester. Our Bard of the Eternal City tells us:

> It was once the site of a sacred grove with Druidic associations, which local people held in awe even in the nineteenth century. . . . Its vague but old-established reputation as a sacred spot and its position on the three-county junction suggest that the Whiteleafed Oak was a significant point in the sacred geography of archaic Britain. . . . And it is delightfully appropriate that it should be found to stand at the hub of the circle of Perpetual Choirs, for at the cathedrals of Hereford, Worcester and Gloucester, the counties which meet together at the Whiteleafed Oak, are held today the famous musical festivals of the Three Choirs.

> The circle of Perpetual Choirs must be older than any structure existing today, older than the present Stonehenge which was built about four thousand

years ago on a site of far earlier sanctity. Both the plan of Magnesia and the New Jerusalem foundation-plan at Glastonbury can be seen as restorations, designed to reinvigorate the tradition of sacred science; and it may be that Stonehenge had the same purpose. Here one is limited to speculation, but it is at least conceivable that when its builders erected the Stonehenge sarsen circle with its mean radius of 50.4 ft, they were aware that this dimension reflected the 504-furlong radius of the Perpetual Choir circle on the scale of 1:6600; and they may have constructed their Temple as part of a revival programme, aimed at restoring the musical enchantment with which the ancient bards held a whole country in harmony with the heavens.

So I end my history. The answer to the question 'Who owns Stonehenge?' is now clear. It belongs to the world, we who live in this sacred Isle are its custodians and we should be its users, not for trivia, not for political ideology, and not for profit, but for the encouragement of the youth of the world in their strivings to better the world for their children. . .

STONEHENGE BELONGS TO THE FUTURE.

CHAPTER FIVE

STONEHENGE:
ACADEMIC CLAIMS
AND RESPONSIBILITIES

Peter Fowler

For the purposes of this chapter, I first cast myself in the role of 'Establishment Man'. What are the claims on Stonehenge of this creature in contemporary terms? The answer is very much as it has been ever since the emergence of scientifically-based scholarship in post-Renaissance times.

ACADEMIC FREEDOM

As a Professor, I am contractually obliged to teach, research and administrate. The last need not concern us here to any degree, though it occupies much of my time. In what is left, but much more importantly in principle, I claim the right to teach whatever I like about Stonehenge, or anything else relevant to my field, in whatever manner I choose. Such a view may not be fashionable in certain government and educational circles at the moment; but essentially that principle is what 'academic freedom' is all about. Not that it is specifically 'academic'. It is the same freedom exercised by my co-authors here, some of them writing, without editorial constraint, in a vein which I would regard as 'self-deluding', or even mischievous nonsense.

For me, controlling factors are my own conscience and abilities, together with the pressures of 'peer review' in the widest sense, rather than the dictates of any particular faction. If in practice this means telling students that modern druids are bogus and ley-liners are loonies, so be it: I do not pretend to a monopoly of knowledge but I do regard it as a prime duty to make students think. They can judge for themselves and that is the critical objective. Whether I chose to help them arrive at that blissful state by laying out the range of evidence in a neutral fashion or by blasting them with opinionated prejudice really is a matter for my judgement, as it is for any teacher, depending on the circumstances of the group or individual being taught.

As a responsible teacher, however, I would hope that overall, as distinct from any one occasion, my approach would be somewhat more temperate than the views exemplified above and that I would at least be capable of indicating my biases when being intemperate. In fact, in using Stonehenge recently as a case-study about attitudes to the heritage, part of my material was what I hope was a fair representation of the views expressed in Paul Devereux's chapter here (rather to the students' surprise) and one of our visiting lecturers on the same course was Tim Sebastian who was naturally given complete freedom to say whatever he liked. And that occasion, precisely because it aired views about which personally I harbour certain reservations, illustrates my first major point about Stonehenge and much else. It is quite simply that the principle of academic freedom is a very real freedom, a privilege we are lucky to enjoy in British society but nevertheless one which is fundamental to the understanding of a very great deal including Stonehenge. And this freedom extends in all directions. In claiming it

54 The classic view out from the centre of Stonehenge, past the Heel stone towards the direction of midsummer sunrise.

55 *Above* During the 1960s, freedom of access meant freedom to trample, and turned the centre of Stonehenge into a mess of mud.
Right In the early 1980s, the centre was closed, and visitors are confined instead to a tarmac surface some distance from the stones. They are still free to walk round the outer circle; the photograph shows the wear their myriad footprints inflict on the site.

professorially, in no way am I claiming it as an exclusive privilege; rather am I pointing out that what I claim as my right extends equitably to others with views about the monument. In my case, however, to my exercise of the right is added the duty to examine critically others' views and, as appropriate, support or demolish them in the interests of 'Truth' (and not, unlike Pilate, in jest).

The first right I claim, therefore, is to teach what and how I like about Stonehenge in ways that I professionally judge to be most appropriate. In so doing, I am responsible to my conscience, my students, my subject and my University Council (probably in that order, though that is another matter). I am not responsible to druids, other mono-model pushers, the official guide book – or, in 1989, the dictates of a possibly doctrinaire government as implied by parts of the 1988 Education Act (though of course there is no doubt that legislation can *legally* inhibit my exercise of the principle of academic freedom while I remain in university employ).

ACCESS

As a teacher, I also regard myself as having a right of reasonable access to the monument and its environs for educational purposes. Though prepared to accept some constraints on access (fig. 55), because I am also imbued with the conservation ethic and would wish my students to be so too, I would equally argue it to be the duty of the managers of the site for the time being to provide that reasonable educational access now, whatever their long-term plans and objectives. I do not regard Stonehenge as 'belonging' in a general sense to any one person or institution or cult, though I acknowledge that in a strictly legal sense it is owned by a corporation. That corporation is in fact the Government which accepted, on behalf of the nation, the monument as a gift. For practical purposes, the owner has passed the management of the site to another body after nearly 80 years during which it was looked after by a government department. Now, the Historic Buildings and Monuments Commission, inheriting an unhappy situation resulting from decades of mismanagement, has to cope with present demands, including mine for educational access, while addressing the major problems arising from its policy decision to improve the care and presentation of Stonehenge (Chapter 7).

My point here is that, whatever the management and practical problems of running the site, an educational right of access is, in my view, a high priority. This is not because I personally should be privileged but because the conjunction of a particular group of students in my company can happen but once. It must be a reasonable expectation on their part that they can visit one of Britain's major monuments in the company of their Professor as an important part of their education, basically at a time to suit their course requirements rather than one dictated by site-management convenience.

As it happens, I visited Stonehenge in 1988 with eight students taking my 'heritage' course as one of their third-year special subjects. The students were duly set down at Larkhill to walk across the downs from the north, appraising *en route* the proposed site for the new reception centre and the approaches to the monument to be offered in future to the visitor. I drove round to Stonehenge, left the minibus in the sordid car park, and met the students; I walked with them across the road to talk about some of the detail of the site and its management (from outside the fence, I might add, since by common consent we agreed it was not worth paying the entrance fee for our purposes). I was in full flood, when we heard a voice saying, 'Can you move out of the way?' Not registering that this meant me, I continued; at which the request was repeated more loudly and peremptorily. Pausing, I turned, and saw across the road an American male, plus female and camera, doing a fair imitation of a one-armed breast-stroke swimmer, clearly intimating that we should move out of his way so he could take his photograph. This I politely declined to do, saying that I was in the middle of teaching. I turned back to my students, when we all heard a word zapped across the road: 'Ass-hole'.

I have been called many things in my life, but not until that moment had my persona been reduced to such an anatomical detail. I continued talking for a few seconds, then, asking my students to excuse me, I turned and, hands in jacket pockets and risking life and limb on a busy road, I walked slowly across to the opposite verge. Pressing right up against him, I enquired, eye-ball to eye-ball, whether he would care to repeat his descriptor. He did. This was an awkward situation, since I had rather committed myself to confrontation. For a split second I reviewed my only realistic alternatives in the circumstances – a short-arm jab to the solar plexus or a knee to the groin – but fortunately it was time enough for my tourist to back off. I suspect it was the relief from tension that enabled me to draw on an unsuspected wealth of vernacular Anglo-Saxon in which to articulate some pertinent observations on the origin of his parents, himself and his nation. His last words as he was shepherded away by his companion were to the effect that 'asshole' in the States did not mean what it did in England – a weak parting shot, I thought, but I knew it to be true, so let it pass and returned somewhat shaken by my own potential for violence, to my students. 'As I was saying. . . .'

The relevance here of this true incident is twofold. First, I marvel once again at the power of 'the Stones' to arouse passion, potentially violent. Only this time it was me, not hippies or travellers or police. And it was not the epithet that incensed me: rather was it being expected while on serious business to get out of the way for a tourist, and a foreign one at that, for a trivial reason. Indeed the incident could have been staged and scripted for the title of this book. Who indeed owns Stonehenge? – an English professor and his students using it quite properly for educational purposes or an American tourist wanting to take his photograph? My claim is professional, nationalistic and, to an extent, assumed; the American's was personal, international and, probably, assumed too. We both sought to exercise proprietorial rights of a kind and were taken aback when they were challenged.

RESEARCH

As an academic, I also claim access to the Stonehenge corpus for purposes of research, i.e., to advance knowledge (fig. 56). By the 'Stonehenge corpus' I mean not just the monument and its environs which public attention concentrates on but more particularly the academic base which supports our understanding of Stonehenge. After all, Stonehenge and its surrounds have not just come to prominence in our own day; as outlined in Chapter 1, it has a very respectable tradition of scholarly work upon it over at least four centuries. As a result, the 'corpus' now consists of many artefacts and voluminous records together forming the archive both of the archaeology itself and of the many people and institutions who have concerned themselves with the monument and its area (fig. 57). This archive provides the already-observed research base from which new work can proceed; but like all archives, it needs curating and it needs to be active in the sense of providing access to it as well as remaining open to receive new materials. I expect that archive to be curated professionally, and I expect the costs of such permanent curation to be met, as a matter of duty and pride, primarily by the public purse through rates and taxes.

That is an expectation which would be questioned by some in the currently fashionable political climate but that cannot alter the fact that 'soft' money is no basis for long-term, indeed permanent, curation. In practice, of course, let it be said before the monetarists yell this proposition down that much of the archive has for a century or more been assembled and looked after entirely from provision made by private money. It came from the founders of the museums in Salisbury

56 This eighteenth-century scheme, by William Stukeley, of 'The manner of laying on the impost at Stonehenge', no longer fits our ideas, but it is not an absurdity. *Watercolour in the Bodleian Library, Oxford.*

and Devizes and above all from the 'amateur' individual members of the Wiltshire Archaeological and Natural History Society, year in and year out, with their annual subscriptions since 1854.

The contributions of the rate-payer, through the local authorities, are a relatively recent phenomenon; though now they are financially crucial. They nevertheless contribute to a mixed economy, for the reliance upon individual subscriptions and donations continues. This means, and happily, that someone like myself – and I am typical of many in this respect – contributes several times over: formerly as a rate-payer living in Wiltshire, and still as a tax-payer, unlike some other contemporary claimants on Stonehenge; as a member of the County Society, of The National Trust, and of English Heritage, paying my annual subscriptions; and as a visitor contributing in a tiny way my mite of expenditure. In other words, contributions to the cost of the archive, and indeed of looking after the site itself, come from a variety of sources, from income generated on-site and in museums as well as from statutory bodies and private donations, and it is right that this should be so, provided that impersonal public money underpins the system. So, I have a financial stake in the 'Stonehenge corpus', enhancing my claim to have access to it as of right; though here again my claim is neither

57 Excellent recording is essential to the research responsibility. Stuart Piggott (right) draws during the excavations of the 1950s.
Photograph by Austin Underwood.

monopolistic nor exclusive. I expect to share the resource, indeed would be disappointed if my interest existed in a social vacuum. I therefore gladly accept that multiple use of the resource will put some constraint on my particular needs and convenience as an academic (fig. 58).

STEWARDSHIP

Within certain constraints, then, my claims are to teach and to research and to have access to Stonehenge as of right as a professional teacher and academic. I have another claim too, in both those capacities and also as a citizen. This goes back to the matter already touched on, namely the custodianship of Stonehenge itself. I expect it to be looked after properly and I think I have a right to expect that such will be the case in the hands of whoever has the responsibility for its conservation. Like many others, I am far from convinced that this responsibility has been properly discharged in recent decades. Admittedly, the monument itself is still there and it has survived various attacks up it; but its immediate and medium-range environment has deteriorated visibly and physically in the time that I have known it. Maybe it has now passed its nadir, not least because the authorities, having made such energetic and costly efforts to defend it in recent years, are now in self-defence bound to show that that which they have defended was worth the effort. My fourth claim for adequate preservation and presentation of the 'Stones' and their surrounding context meanwhile stands.

It goes without saying that these several claims as of right carry with them equally strong obligations to contribute as well as consume, to give as well as take. To make the point is of course to articulate a traditional, even old-fashioned Establishment line, but it is one commonly held by academics and particularly by archaeologists in relation to the national and local heritage. It contrasts in its altruism and public spirit with the motivation and efforts of nearly all other consumers of the Stonehenge phenomenon, whether they be latter-day druids, ley-liners, wallies, festivalites or tourists. The contribution of such to the well-being of Stonehenge as a resource, intellectual and physical, is at best question-able and is characteristically erosive, introverted and self-gratifying. I appreciate they do not see it that way, but I am dealing with reality, not wish-fulfilment.

In the past, archaeological excavators, along with others, have also taken away from Stonehenge's integrity. Excavators, for example, have impaired evidence below ground in their quest for understanding; similarly, curio-collectors, in this case the geological equivalent of barrow-robbing antiquarians, hammered chips off the old stones. At least most of the old-time excavators were genuinely trying to find out more about Stonehenge; the damage caused through inadequate technique then was, as we can now see, a price deemed worth paying at the time in terms of both research and controlled restoration. Now, however, ethical attitudes within the fast-growing profession of archaeology have significantly changed. We, like others, can and do question some of what has been done in the past in the name of 'science'. It is perfectly obvious that, in archaeology as in other emergent sciences, mistakes have been made. Furthermore this applies much closer to our own time in the even younger field of 'interpretation' i.e. seeking to put over to a mass, lay audience the nature and significance of a site in such a way that the visit becomes an individual 'experience' (I use the jargon without comment, having recently learnt that I cannot simply go to the pub for a drink any longer because the brewery company wishes to sell me a 'leisure experience').

Nevertheless, despite the mistakes, archaeology would argue that it has learnt quickly from experience by being sensitive both to the needs of the resource and to the currents in contemporary society. It is accepted that Stonehenge needs no further excavation at the moment; archaeology is not the threat (fig. 59). To say as much is a major contribution of the late 1980s to the monument. Whatever other claims are made of and for it, Stonehenge is now primarily an archaeological site; yet, in a spirit of academic and professional responsibility which characterized recent debate about the justification for further excavation at Sutton Hoo and at Castlerigg stone circle, archaeologists themselves have properly imposed a self-denying ordinance.

The reason is easy to identify, though other interest-groups seem incapable of recognizing it; rather do they prefer, in their own self-interest if not actual ignorance, to continue characterizing archaeology and archaeologists in anachronistic clichés. All the same, the fact is that a generation has now passed in which archaeology's main concern, following the *diktat* of the great Mortimer Wheeler, has been with people rather than things; and its interests have moved wider still, as a matter of routine, into environmental and social elucidation. In that context, it is simply unlikely that further excavation has much to contribute to knowledge at the moment. Therefore, let us leave it alone. It is far more important to sort out its management, firstly to prolong its existence as a scientific resource and, secondly, to make the site and area available to contemporary use consonant with the primary objective.

STONEHENGE AND I

Let me illustrate my remark about a positive, caring attitude from responsible academia with an autobiographical note. Contributions from other archaeologists would vary in detail but my experience is typical, even if this sounds like archetypal 'Establishment Man'. As a member of Council, and chairman of the Archaeology Committee, of the Wiltshire Archaeological and Natural History Society in the 1960s and 1970s, I spent countless voluntary hours on Stonehenge affairs. We were, 20 years ago, much concerned with the deteriorating appearance of and facilities at the site as tourist numbers increased; we were appalled at the archaeological damage being allowed to happen on the thousands of acres around the henge which had been bought by public subscription and handed over to the National Trust *for preservation*, yet were being cultivated just like any other downland; and there were many meetings of a Joint Working Party with representatives from Salisbury Museum exploring the very good chance there then was for a new Stonehenge Museum. That nothing came of so much

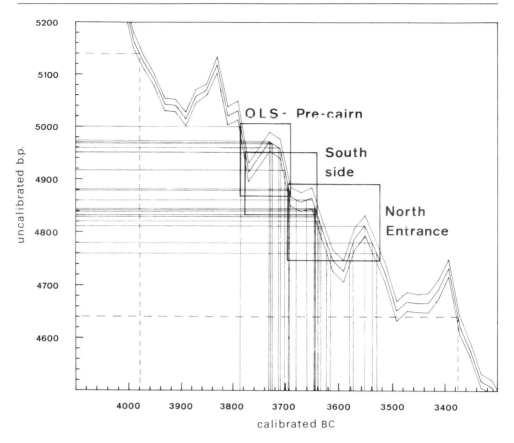

58 A new chronology of Stonehenge is likely to be presented, in the archaeological literature, in this way: the mass of lines on a diagram expresses our knowledge of the date of the Hazleton long cairn in the Cotswolds, 1987.
Courtesy of Alan Saville.

good-willed endeavour – as with so much else connected with Stonehenge – does not discount the considerable effort involved.

Later, one of my first tasks in 1979 as the new Secretary to the Royal Commission on Historical Monuments (England) was to see through the press *Stonehenge and Its Environs*, out of the myriad of Stonehenge publications this century, one of the half-dozen or so significant books on the Stonehenge phenomenon. From 1979 too, I sat on the now defunct Ancient Monuments Board and, during 1983–6, on its successor Ancient Monuments Advisory Committee. One of the many concerns of both bodies was, needless to say, Stonehenge, then boiling up rather interestingly as the whole question of its presentation and its use came to a head. I was therefore party to the discussions and, ultimately, to the decision which closed Stonehenge in the mid-summers of

1985 and 1986. In parallel, from 1982 I was (and still am) on the Council of The National Trust, its governing body under Act of Parliament. I was therefore, reluctantly but nevertheless, party to the decision to ban the festival from Trust land near Stonehenge each year from 1985 to 1989. 'Establishment Man' indeed.

The point of detailing this personal involvement is, however, to illustrate how one academic tried to contribute, partly voluntarily, partly professionally, but always within the concept and framework of public service. Others were doing likewise, trying to tackle a real-life situation which had arisen out of issues somewhat removed from teaching and research but in the resolution of which a certain amount of archaeological know-how might be relevant. As is discussed elsewhere in this book, however, the issues went far beyond academic ones. They were created outside academia, and indeed far from Stonehenge itself, by a growing public demand and, probably more significant than the quantitative problem, by a changing expectation of the 'Stonehenge experience' and by a changing perception of the function and meaning of Stonehenge in the late twentieth century. As always a reflection of contemporaneity rather than just an 'Ancient Monument', Stonehenge from the 1970s onwards closely mirrored eddies, then stronger undercurrents, in our own society. Whether I wear my public servant or professorial hat, as an individual I am a member of that democratic society; and in that personal capacity, I looked on Stonehenge in the 1980s and could have wept.

Personally, of course I questioned, to put it mildly, the need for and the nature of the police action taken in 1985 and 1989. I trembled with shame when fellow-members of The National Trust who had been subject to the 1985 police action were denied a fair hearing at the Trust's Annual General Meeting that autumn by a hostile and, to my mind, perhaps deeply disturbed assembly. I have hated seeing Stonehenge entangled in barbed-wire, the parade-ground of militarism, the symbol of elitism, the denial of what I choose to teach, the antithesis of what I believe our heritage should be to those who wish to participate in it. Might is not right for Stonehenge but, equally, neither is mass invasion. Clearly something went badly wrong, an unhelpful observation but one leading to the question 'why?'

THE STATUTORY CONTEXT

Essentially the generalized answer is that England's land-owning-based administrative system, stemming from its legal framework, was unable to be sufficiently flexible in circumstances it was not designed to meet. The denial, 'Thou shalt not', is built into it as the predetermined response. I fully accept, however, that from a different point of view, this negative drawing of a line could be seen as precisely what the system was intended to do: a time-gaining mechanism to hold a position defensively while a new set of circumstances was appraised. From this

viewpoint the system can be judged to have worked. A defensive position was successfully held and time for consideration was gained in circumstances where some of the customer-led demands of the resource were unreasonable. Indeed, it would have been irresponsible, and in legal fact statutorily impossible, for those charged for the time being with the stewardship of Stonehenge and its surrounds in the long-term scientific and public interest to have acceded to such demands just on the nod.

That point lay behind the apparently po-faced, un-understanding, reactionary postures adopted by the two main institutions charged with looking after the monument and its landscape. Though both the Historic Buildings and Monuments Commission and The National Trust are independent bodies, both have statutory responsibilities laid upon them by Act of Parliament. Given those, and the circumstances of real threat to the physical well-being of a part of the common heritage with whose long-term conservation they are charged, I do not see how the two bodies could have taken any other decisions. Their prime responsibility was to protect that with which they were charged and not in the first instance to solve the problems of a well-known social phenomenon – mass trespass – aggravated by tensions particular to the circumstances of the 1980s. Given their brief, their job was to cope with the consequences of that phenomenon as they impinged on their responsibility.

Similarly and concurrently, The National Trust has decided to refuse Ministry of Defence demands on inalienable land needed to enhance the radar-tracking capability along the Welsh coast. The Trust responsibility is to protect coast-line designated as 'of natural beauty' and accepted by it for that reason, and not, so it argues, to involve itself in the primary decision as to whether or not the land is actually needed for the defence of the realm. That is for the Government to decide, and the place for debate on the matter in those terms is Parliament and not in the Council of the Trust. Neither Government nor Parliament were averse to giving their attention to both the causes and the consequences of the social phenomenon which focussed on Stonehenge in the mid 1980s, though, quite properly, despite much adverse comment in the media, there was little criticism at Westminster of the decisions themselves made by the Commission and the Trust. Both bodies are in business to make such decisions where and when necessary purely on conservation grounds. It is most important to draw the distinction between the defensible decisions as such and their executive consequences, largely in the hands of others.

59 *Opposite* In 1979 a telephone cable was laid along the road by Stonehenge, through a very precious fragment of the deposits that still survive round the Heel stone. Salvage work provided evidence for an unknown stone, once the twin to the Heel Stone. Salvage archaeology in advance of the visitors' tarmac path had better cause and made less damage.

Maybe the Acts need changing, maybe the implementation and consequences of those decisions were less than happy. Nevertheless, the fact is that at the time, and still, the thrust of legal provisions emphasizes the priority of physical preservation, and quite specifically of archaeological remains and 'places of historic interest'. It follows that the impact of any actions in, or contemporary functions of, the Stonehenge cultural complex must be subordinate to that statutory priority. Doubtless that seems a stuffy, unimaginative Establishment point of view, a case of the academic hanging on to the legal *status quo* as a matter of expediency simply because it happens, through its historical development, to be biased in favour of archaeological preservation. The only answer I can give to that charge is that, bias and historical accident notwithstanding, legislation and administrative procedures which give a priority to the protection of the primary material in the field, the resource which has fortuitously survived millennia of wear and tear into our own times, and which is in addition absolutely irreplaceable – such a system has to be seen as fundamentally correct as a matter, not of expediency, but of principle.

Those who disagree with such a view fortunately live, in Britain anyway, in a democracy. They can take perfectly legal steps to try to change the provisions, indeed the biases, of the Acts of Parliament. If people want to turn Stonehenge into a fair-ground, if they want the surrounding landscape to be turned into car-parks and festival-camps, if society wants to consume this bit of its heritage in one generation and pass on to its successors a relict landscape as a monument to our greed rather than the monument inherited from our ancestors, then all that has to be done is for the Acts of Parliament to be changed. I am quite sure that future Commissioners and Councils charged with different responsibilities under new legislation would be as conscientious in the discharge of their new duties as they have been and are in the execution of their present ones.

ACADEMIC RESPONSIBILITY

The *academic* responsibilities on people like myself in the present vibrant, if unsatisfactory, situation are quite clear. As an archaeologist and conservationist, my first responsibility is precisely to see that the Acts, now with a century of conceptual wisdom behind them, are indeed enforced. They are specifically designed to promote the long-term survival of one of our most important national resources, our cultural heritage. To say as much is not to grovel before the contemporary altar of tourist-led heritage-hype but merely to reflect what many, academics and craftsmen for example, have for long believed. Archaeologists think long-term anyway, so they in particular can afford to stand back from current fads, to see the ebb and flow of attitudes towards and use of 'the past' in the widest sense. They can appreciate that the significant objective is to try to ensure the existence into the future of outstanding and representative landscapes, structures and objects.

That is the strategy. Meanwhile, at the practical level in our own day, the real challenge is to participate in the creative management of the remains of the past by balancing the long-term objective with the claims of contemporary society. In practice, those claims exist at two levels: on the ground and in the mind. As an academic and teacher, I am as involved with the latter – and hence my involvement with this book – as I am in fairly obvious ways with the former.

What people think and feel about Stonehenge now is as interesting, as important, and certainly more immediate than what we can study of human thoughts about antiquity in the eighteenth century, or what we think people might think about their past in the twenty-first century. Given my academic, scientific, conservationist priorities, it nevertheless matters enormously to me that as many of my contemporaries as so wish should be able to take the 'Stonehenge experience' in their own individual way. They should be able to think as they like on its meaning, both for themselves as individuals and in general. Such a position inevitably takes us back to consideration of the highly controversial subject of 'interpretation'. Access is one thing; 'access to what?' is a question begging several others.

A claim I make, and a responsibility I accept, is that the public presentation of Stonehenge must be *founded* on scientific observation (fig. 60). Many facts about the monument and the area have been compiled over the centuries; many of them are now unrecordable again – the evidence has disappeared – but they are enshrined in the 'Stonehenge corpus', the academic memory bank. As a professional academic I have to insist that that corpus be taken into account in 'interpreting' the complex to the public; indeed, personally I would go further and argue that the presentation has to be based upon not just what is known but more fundamentally upon that rational approach to the past which has so character-ized west European scholarship since the Renaissance. Not only is that right in principle, but to do anything less or otherwise would be to betray the past of the study of the past and, in all fairness, the legitimate expectation of the visitors.

Again, to claim as much is not to claim exclusivity or a monopoly of interpretative rectitude and certainly not to paint a scenario in which scholarship provides all answers to all people for all time. But the foundation of presentation must be scholarship. That said, and recognizing that these are different issues, within the presentation of course there must be room for alternative views and uses, for they too are interesting and in any case have their place within the history of Stonehengiana; and similarly, to insist on the academic foundations is to say nothing about the techniques of presentation which, given their basic terms of reference, can and perhaps should be as modish as technology, design and finance allow.

What would be wrong, however, would be if the whole of the presentation

135

60 Holes cut down to the solid chalk are the foundation of Stonehenge and also the foundation of our scientific knowledge of Stonehenge. On the evidence of neat holes like this, and their precise recording, depends such truth about Stonehenge as exists in the apparatus of ideas about it.

were based, for example, on the presumption that Stonehenge were a computer or a temple of the Druids. It would also be unacceptable if the whole presentation concentrated on impressing the visitor with media-hype for its own sake on 'the medium is the message' principle. Stonehenge is far too significant to be marketed merely as a meaning-of-the-month or as the platform for the psychedelia of the specious-interest groups. Its interpretation must allow for a very wide range of personal approaches and reactions but the starting point must be reason. Where people end up in their private explorations from there must be left to them. There is no ultimate 'truth', no certainty, to be rammed down their throats. Archaeology can say a lot, and other approaches can contribute to the interest, but no one knows what Stonehenge 'means', not least because meaning is ultimately a personal choice and no amount of scientifically-based 'reason' is going to change the mind of the bigot or the ignoramus.

Most people are ignorant of what is actually known about Stonehenge; some choose to stay that way. One justification for the principle of academic freedom is that, as far as matters academic in this field are concerned, the scholar knows best. By this is meant that he has dutifully acquainted himself with *all* relevant information, and formed a judgement on the basis of it. This is not to say that the judgement is absolutely correct, but to assert that such a judgement is the best-informed and impartial interpretation available for the time being. Non-scholars make great play of the ways that interpretations change through time, and of different archaeologists offering different interpretations of Stonehenge at the same time. To denigrate this characteristic of the nature of scholarship is simply to exhibit ignorance of the ways in which knowledge is formed and transformed: change as such does not diminish the status of knowledge or the methods of scholarship, for both are concerned with change as they edge hopefully towards better understanding – and the process very definitely includes going inadvertently up blind alleys and quite simply getting things wrong. Not so for the person who knows from the start what the 'truth' is: he merely has to select the evidence to fit his 'truth' and either remain ignorant of the rest or discard it as irrelevant. Further, his 'truth' is absolute: it is revealed, and its nature is permanent, the very antithesis of the rational, scientific approach embraced within the concept of scholarship.

Archaeology, as an approach to the past, is about scholarship. Many of its practitioners strive to be scholarly; some succeed. Their views about the past, about Stonehenge, are simply of a different and, I have to assert, a superior nature from the often enthusiastic and very plausible quasi- and pseudo-truths offered by the non-scholarly penumbra encircling the academic heartland.

Attractive though the alternatives are, they are the soft options. Life is not simple; nor was it in the past. Explanation is inherently likely to be complex, understanding it is likely to be difficult, for we are trying to recover complicated and dynamic processes. There is no simple explanation for as complex and long-lived a structure as Stonehenge, any more than there is for the Houses of Parliament or the growth of London. Both are well recorded, but new evidence comes to light, old information takes on new significance, interpretation changes and, perhaps above all, each new generation assesses its received past and creates a new one. But at any one time, the basis of the most reliable interpretation will be the real evidence, the observed facts and the archive; 'truth' relates to this, carefully taken into account in the light of new information and more modern ways of studying and thinking. This is the way to better understanding, despite the alluring temptations of cabalistic, secretive, emotional approaches with their overt simplicity, crude disregard for inconvenient evidence and tendency to supply 'evidence' where it is lacking. All of this means that the future of Stonehenge lies with archaeology and the scholarship it generates.

Archaeology's criteria are scientific, well-founded and, within the world-wide rules of the academic game, testable, defensible and, to an intellectually agreeable extent, successful. They have produced a portfolio of images of a prehistoric past where there was none, without in any way producing a comprehensive understanding. But then, neither the discipline nor its practitioners have a monopoly of intuition, sensitivity, humanity or wisdom.

Our role, as I see it, is to conserve; to try to be learned; to try to expand the frontiers of understanding, by research and by listening to the Sebastians and Devereux on our flanks; to formulate and review continuously as balanced a judgement as possible in the light of *all* available evidence, eschewing the advocacy of any one particular line, ley or otherwise; and to communicate the results of our considerations, including our uncertainties and the exposure of the bogus, to the public. In relation to our fellow-men, unlike some other groups with claims on Stonehenge, *we* are in a position of trust. I hope it is not arrogant to claim that for, as a professional, I believe it ultimately to be the basis of my position. I may or may not enjoy my archaeology, but I am not playing at it. Furthermore, I believe the concept of being in a position of public trust to be particularly sensitive now in view of the single most significant development in our communal relationship to our past that has happened during my career. I refer, not to radiocarbon dating, not to the late-lamented 'new' archaeology, not to the development of excavation wizardry, nor to the application of many scientific techniques to the study of the past. That most significant development is the realization that the past is not merely what has happened but is also to be understood as part of 'current affairs'.

CHAPTER SIX

STONEHENGE
IN A DEMOCRATIC
SOCIETY

Peter Fowler

A Stonehenge free festival was first held in summer 1974, near the Stones. Where other festivals of the flower-power era faded away, the Stonehenge festival grew, still unofficial and with no formal organizer, but in the 1980s becoming a larger, more structured affair that took possession of the field, on National Trust land, that lies across the main road to the north and west of Stonehenge for a couple of weeks around the midsummer solstice. By 1984, its eleventh year, the festival had established an uneasy *modus vivendi* with the National Trust and English Heritage, who wished it would not happen but felt they could not stop it. In early May, defences were built around Stonehenge of tangled barbed wire, as if for a First World War trench. The festival-goers did not storm the fortifications, but entered the usual field, built the stage, and settled down to festival. The authorities did not intervene much, nor the police who watched from a mobile police station in the Stonehenge car-park. Some of the festival came into Stonehenge at dawn on the midsummer morning, along with the Druids who celebrate then. More came in the afternoon, when the Druids were done. The festival lingered on in its field until July, and left the place in the kind of squalor you might expect from mass camping without sanitation or firewood supplies. Holes had been dug for latrines and ovens, young trees broken down, fences broken. Clearing up cost £20,000.

In 1985 the festival was stopped, the first year of an intermittent battle between the official side and 'the Convoy' – the group of people, often travelling together, who wish to make a Stonehenge festival – a battle which continues.

In a book of diverse views, this chapter touches on some common ground. We are all concerned about the place of Stonehenge in contemporary society. As a contemporary phenomenon occasioning aggravation in public and of national concern, Stonehenge refuses to go away. It has become part of the cycle of the English summer along with Wimbledon, Henley and the Lords Test Match.

61 The free Stonehenge, as visitors experienced it two centuries ago, alone on the unfenced turf of the Wiltshire downland. Engraving, about 1800.

62 'Ancient and modern: motor cars at Stonehenge, Easter 1899.' Magazine illustration from two years before a fall of stones caused Stonehenge to be fenced and an admission fee charged.

63 Duties of the Stonehenge policemen, early in the century, seem to involve some mild confrontation. Date and circumstances unknown.

'Convoy is Set for its Summer Ritual' said the *Sunday Times* on 31 May 1987, suggesting a fatalistic routine like 'England Batting Collapse Again'.

The story of Stonehenge in the 1980s seems to all of us too remarkable and too disturbing to be forgotten as yet another curious affair now relegated to yellowing press cuttings. In any case, 1989 showed that the issues not only live but continue to develop, out-of-doors and indoors. For example, in November 1989, the Wiltshire police were ordered in the High Court in London to disclose documents relating to their actions near Stonehenge in 1985. We can be confident that the Stonehenge phenomenon will be alive in the 1990s. Whether it will be as violent remains to be seen.

Though the issues are complex, not least because of their symbolism, three are fundamental.

Legally, Stonehenge has been an Ancient Monument for just over a century. This status gives a priority to preservation; that is, the physical well-being of the structure and its environs is the prime duty of its custodians, English Heritage.

64 Druid ceremony, 1923, in the centre of the Temple. Celebrants in white with a respectful congregation.
Photograph from library of Roger Viollet, Paris.

This status implies that the site is 'dead'; its original purposes finished, its future is as a preserved relic, an archaism for the delectation of visitors and scholars. In such circumstances, the use of the site by large gatherings of people, not visitors in the tourist sense, nor scholars, clearly has to be carefully considered – simply because they are not what the law envisages as the site's function.

Yet many people now see Stonehenge primarily as a living, religious place – indeed, more as a 'temple' (fig. 66). The majority in a secular society finds it difficult to sympathize with this view; far easier to ridicule it. But whatever the objections – the 'religion' is pagan, unauthentic, self-deluding, silly – the sincerity of the present-day religious beliefs centred on Stonehenge must, it seems to me, be accepted. However correct management of the monument may be in secular terms (fig. 67), it will be defiling the 'holy', and be seen as 'unreasonable', from a 'New Age' religious point of view (fig. 68). (One feels a comparable unease in those British cathedrals which are so full of tourists and which have become so concerned with the commercial aspects of their activity that they no longer have an atmosphere that is primarily religious.)

65 Ring-a-roses at dawn, 1956, when crowds were good-humoured, and climbing on the stones just the thing.
Photograph by Austin Underwood.

66 The Druid ceremony as it is felt it should be, in an atmospheric recent painting.

Furthermore, Stonehenge has become entangled with one of the major social issues of our time, the question of access, in the sense of physical access to property. Who has the right of access to the Stonehenge, and when? Who has the right to deny that access, and why? Such questions raise matters of some import: the extent of police powers in a democracy, the extent of personal freedom in a democracy, and whether there is room, literally as well as conceptually, for people 'of no fixed abode' in a bureaucratically-based, property-owning and, above all, settled society.

We do not think that Stonehenge and all it has come to symbolize over the last 15 years is a straightforward matter, to be sorted out by tried administrative procedures, supported, as necessary, by legitimized force. One reason it has dragged on, year after year, is because traditional attitudes, working by precedent, cannot cope with the complex of forces and interests, psychological as well as physical. The Stonehenge conflict, at any one time or simultaneously, has consisted, depending on one's point of view, of law and order *versus* chaos, goodies *versus* baddies, Thatcher's Britain *versus* the dispossessed in (and

67 The Druid solstice ceremony, these last few years, has been held   if at all – on the tarmac road by Stonehenge, with a crowd pressing in, and lines of police, with coiled barbed wire behind, separating the Druids from their Temple.
Photograph by Christopher Chippindale.

68 In this official army photograph, Crown Copyright Reserved and issued by Public Relations at HQ United Kingdom Land Forces, Salisbury, a flight of small military helicopters heads west over Stonehenge, with the Larkhill base and range in the background.
Crown copyright.

drop-outs from) its selfish society, police *versus* brigands, landowners *versus* travellers, scroungers *versus* worthy tax-paying folk, a watery Christianity *versus* a ludicrously romantic paganism, stuffy Establishment *versus* the liberating forces of Light, archaeologists *versus* lunatic fringe, youth *versus* anything. And the atmosphere has often been one of folk devils and the moral panic they may cause.

SOCIAL FORCES

A stimulation to our thinking about Stonehenge as a phenomenon in current affairs was the oral contribution by Tim Malyon to the Southampton conference which first brought us together. These next paragraphs draw heavily on Malyon's material; as a freelance journalist who covered Stonehenge for some years, he speaks with a different and authoritative voice. It was heard once again at the National Trust's AGM in November 1989.

The banning of the Festival in 1985 and 1986 led to at least a thousand arrests, the impounding of over 200 vehicles, including mobile homes, immense inconvenience to the general public and police costs to Wiltshire rate-payers of £1.2 million, for 1985 alone. We do not yet know will wo over? the cost of the police action in 1989.

A 'villain' in the piece, over many years, has been the National Trust, owner of the rolling acres around Stonehenge. Malyon claimed that he had alerted the Trust to the new live interest in Stonehenge in the mid 1970s when the Festival was small and the farmer on whose land it took place, a Trust tenant, would have been willing to lease it. Subsequently the Trust took the public position that it could do nothing to give a Festival site on its own land because none of its tenants was willing to contemplate subletting part of their tenancy for an occasion which, by the late 1970s, had become locally notorious. The continuous failure to find a Festival site has meant that thousands of people each year have concentrated on getting to Stonehenge itself when in all probability, had there been a Festival site somewhere in the general area, they would have been more than happy to go there. As a result, two different issues – of the druidic ceremonies and access to the monument on the one hand, and of a 'free festival' somewhere in the general Stonehenge area on the other – became mixed up. They still are mixed up, with the Druids being banned yet again from Stonehenge for 1990 because of the others who wish to be there.

The Stonehenge Festival, though anarchic, was eventually positive, the only pop festival that actually threw out heroin dealers. The dark side – the damage, the outrage caused to local people – in a sense was the product of official neglect, both in respect of Stonehenge and in forcing the Festival to become illegal.

With many voices raised, the archaeologists were muted. Yet the Festival was abolished in the name of archaeology – on the specific grounds that it was damaging the field archaeology of the Stonehenge area. This above all was the point that the 'festival people' needed to have explained to them, for they were genuinely puzzled why the old festival site was archaeologically unsuitable. The field had been continuously deep-ploughed, indeed used for testing ploughs, into the early 1970s. The alleged fact of 'archaeological damage' was stated, but never demonstrated or explained to those who genuinely needed to know. Yet in 1985 a trench 4.6 m (15 ft) long and 1.8 m (6 ft deep) was dug by the 'official' side in this 'archaeologically sensitive' landscape across the entrance to the Festival field to prevent people going in who might thereafter damage the archaeology; and more digging was done in 1989 for the same reason.

The horrific events of 1985 appalled even a hardened journalist, who has covered many violent events, and who witnessed near Stonehenge scenes of babies being dragged through the jagged glass of broken windows, of buses-as-homes being rammed. This violent débâcle followed a decade with plenty of warning of trouble building up and with lost opportunities for compromise. The Trust's Festival record was snobbish, conceited and blind; or consistently firm and correct – depending on your viewpoint. In the meantime the Festival grew, chaotic and unorganized.

Even in the relatively peaceful events of 1986, about 200 people were arrested and many taken into what was effectively preventive custody so that they caused no trouble. By 1987, however, the Festival was dead, killed by a Government which disliked the 'travelling culture' (fig. 69). There is literally no room for it in Thatcher's conformist Britain. Whatever the illegalities, the inconvenience, even the damage, of the Festival, something spontaneously creative has been destroyed, at least officially; but if its origins really are rooted in political non-conformity, social alienation, in genuinely revivalist trends of personal life-style and religious belief, then however small the minority so affected, the impulse that lies behind the Festival will manifest itself again, elsewhere if not at Stonehenge itself.

69 Stonehenge, solar energy, a tipi and a flower: wall-painting in Camden, north London, about 1986.

CIVIL LIBERTIES

The National Council for Civil Liberties published a booklet in 1986 entitled *Stonehenge: a report into the civil liberties implications of the events relating to the convoys of summer 1985 and 1986*. Here, we can but note a few points which interest us as archaeologists – and citizens. The events associated with Stonehenge led directly to amendments by the Government in a new Public Order Act. That a single Ancient Monument, 4000 and more years old, can in the late twentieth century so agitate so many, including a Prime Minister and her Government, is itself remarkable.

The NCCL booklet sets out the facts behind the moral panic over 'hippies' and the convoy in 1985 and 1986. It examines the powers which the government and local authorities had to prevent the conflict, and criticizes their decision to leave the police to cope. It reveals disturbing new trends in the use of police public-order powers and the extent to which the courts failed to act as impartial arbiters during the conflict. (Since the confrontation, and the writing of the NCCL

70 Clichés of the English summer in the late 1980s: pouring rain and aggravation at Stonehenge.
Cartoon by Oz, from the Southampton Evening Echo, 18 June 1987.

pamphlet, new legal measures have decisively moved the balance of power towards the official side.)

Incompatibility between settled and travelling peoples is central. There really has been no understanding that 'nomads' need a meeting place. This is a genetic, sexual, social, and economic necessity of nomadism. People need to meet to do things, for, with and to each other; they need a meeting-place, related, by common understanding and convenience, to the cycle of their activities, the seasons, and/or the movement of recognized heavenly bodies. Archaeologically we think we see such places in the causewayed enclosures, henge monuments, stone circles and single megaliths of Britain in the fourth to the second millennia BC; anthropologically we know of such places in the recent past; and we can recognize the remnants of the tradition in the Balkans, in Spanish *fiestas*, and in the autumn fairs of the scattered sheep-raising families on the Anglo-Scottish border. Behind the beards and long hair, the bedraggled clothes and nudity, the ramshackle vehicles, and the smells, was a simple, social need unknown to the rest of society and quite incomprehensible to those who live a static life.

Stonehenge, the focus of attention, lies in central, southern England, home of the estate-based lord, the land-owning squirearchy, the independent farmer, the (second?) home-in-the-country commuter, the retired-to-a-bungalow-and-a-large-garden senior citizen – and, in the 1987 General Election, a continuous blue-sea of Tory constituencies. This is no place for nomads, spatially or socio-logically. Every acre is owned, and valued; 'travellers', whatever their mien or motivation, are by definition suspect.

Be that as it may, as the NCCL observes:

the events surrounding the attempt to hold a free festival at Stonehenge in June, 1985 and 1986, raised varied and important issues of civil liberty. These include a conflict between the civil liberties of the convoy to live in the way they wish and the social and economic rights of farmers . . . to earn a living from the land.

The NCCL sees the affair in these terms:

Unfortunately for reason and compromise, the background to the convoy is a 'moral panic' in which all travellers are identified as part of a unified whole, 'the convoy', and characterized as medieval brigands, carriers of AIDS or hepatitis. In this report we briefly examine some of these allegations. NCCL observers report that the backgrounds of the travellers in the convoy are as many and as varied as in an equivalent cross-section of settled people. Some travel with the convoy only at weekends or holidays, others have had a nomadic lifestyle for eight or more years. They are classed as 'hippies' but many are too young to have been part of the San Francisco generation. Some travellers have seasonal work, although there are complaints that this is now in short supply, others manufacture artefacts which they sell at local fairs. Some travellers claim social security, others do not. There is no evidence that a higher proportion of travellers with the convoy have criminal convictions than an equivalent cross-section of the settled community. . .

AN OUTLINE OF EVENTS, 1985–9

1985

The build-up to the 1985 festival began early. In March, Wiltshire County Council announced that the A344 around Stonehenge would be blocked off. In April English Heritage, the National Trust and 17 co-plaintiffs applied for a 'precautionary injunction' against 83 named individuals said to represent the 'central element' of those likely to attend.

In May, the Chief Constable of Wiltshire announced that he would have police on stand-by and additional help from neighbouring police forces to prevent the festival from taking place. Razor wire barricades were erected around the Stones. The police began to stop travellers moving through the west of England.

On 31 May, a convoy of 140 vehicles intent on going to a Stonehenge festival and escorted by the police, moved into Wiltshire and camped at Savernake Forest near Marlborough. Police, including a helicopter, surrounded the camp. On 1 June the convoy set off south down the A338 accompanied by the police. Near Parkhouse the convoy was met by a police road block. The trapped convoy, surrounded by police, moved into an adjacent field. The police, in visored helmets, and carrying riot shields, followed, and a pitched battle ensued. Moving away from the police, some convoy vehicles drove on to the next field, planted with beans, where the 'Battle of the Beanfield' took place (figs. 71a and b). The police followed each vehicle until it stopped or crashed. Television cameras saw the occupants of the vehicles, including children, being removed from their travelling homes. The Earl of Cardigan who witnessed the scene said: 'I shall never forget the screams of one woman who was holding up her little baby in a bus with smashed windows. She screamed and screamed at them to stop, but five seconds later 50 men with truncheons and shields just boiled into that bus. It was mayhem, no other word for it.'

Over 500 members of the convoy were arrested and charged with unlawful assembly, obstruction of the police and obstruction of the highway.

After the 'Battle of the Beanfield', the police impounded many of the convoy vehicles. Further charges against some convoy members were preferred when people came to collect their vehicles.

About 100 travelling homes moved from Savernake to Bratton Castle near Westbury and set up a camp.

Two other groups tried to reach Stonehenge in June. A group of 300 walked from Amesbury but were turned back by the police.

71 Stonehenge has been physical on both sides: arrest at the battle of the Beanfield (above), and assault by the public at the midsummer solstice 1988 (right). *Photograph (above) of unknown origin, (right) by John Voos for the* Independent.

The Druids agreed not to go to the Stones at midsummer.

A second fence was erected around Stonehenge with extra guards and dogs, and English Heritage closed it to the public between 20 and 22 June. On 18 June some members of the convoy applied, unsuccessfully, for an injunction barring the police and authorities from preventing people going to Stonehenge. Although Mr Justice Steyn did not grant the injunction, he expressed concern that Special Action Security Force was being used as a vigilante force to guard areas around Stonehenge.

English Heritage and the Ministry of Defence obtained a possession order against travellers camping at Bratton Castle. The Convoy left on 3 July.

That was the end of the affair in 1985, though court hearings ran through the following months, and legal action continues still.

1986

With the experience of 1985 in each party's mind, the 1986 events began with similar preliminaries. English Heritage, the National Trust, and the County Council assembled their legal and physical defences, and the Wiltshire police prepared for the festival convoy to arrive. Ejected from Camel Hill, across the county border in Somerset, the convoy imposed itself on a farmer's land, ruining his grass crop. The convoy became a public issue, and there was a rush of government statements, which noted the weakness of legal defences against trespass of this nature. The convoy moved toward Dorset, and then to the New Forest. The Home Secretary described the convoy as 'a band of medieval brigands who have no respect for the law or the rights of others', and the Prime Minister said that she was 'only too delighted to do anything we can to make life difficult for such things as hippy convoys'. A series of police operations stalled the convoy. On the solstice day a group were allowed to walk along the A344 to the area adjacent to the Stones for the solstice. These included Druids, secular Druids, some local people, the press and about 100 hippies, with about 100 police between the gathering and Stonehenge itself. More police with dogs surrounded the Stones and helicopters circled overhead.

1987

To everyone's relief, the 1987 summer solstice did not see a repeat of the violent scenes of the previous two years. Though the Trust's ban on a Festival was repeated and para-military precautions were taken around 'the Stones', English Heritage agreed to allow limited numbers of invited people into Stonehenge for the solstice dawn on certain conditions. Some sections of the archaeological fraternity were dismayed that members of the Ancient Order of Druids had preferential treatment, on the grounds that their mumbo-jumbo ceremony was 'traditional'. Was this their pay-off for having been 'good boys' in 1986 when they voluntarily cancelled their ceremony?

The winter solstice – not known as an occasion for ceremonies at Stonehenge before – was marked in December 1987 by a happening at 'the Stones' which took English Heritage unawares.

1988

The National Trust confirmed its ban on a Festival on its land, and English Heritage renewed its measures to protect the monument itself; the Wiltshire police made it clear that they did not expect to have a major role. In renewed clashes between some 5000 people and 1300 police, 67 arrests were made (fig. 71, right). For the first time, small gatherings of the Stonehenge type visibly occurred at one or two other prehistoric megalithic sites, notably Castlerigg stone circle in Cumbria. There, while not preventing access, the National Trust with a small police presence insisted on observance of its bye-law that no camping be allowed on its property (here a single field).

1989

After an early statement that they would again intervene, the police started discouraging some people from entering Wiltshire in May. On 9 June the Home Secretary announced a ban on public marches and rallies near Stonehenge. No procession of more than two people was to be permitted within a defined radius of a few miles from Stonehenge – except in the event of a funeral! For three weeks in June all movement into an area of 13 km (8 miles) diameter around Stonehenge was effectively monitored by a 'ring-fence' of manned road blocks. Stonehenge itself was once again 'fortified'.

This year was, however, pretty well peaceful. The constables sat comfortably in the sun outside their road-block tents, or uncomfortably in the sun inside their vans, and spent their time watching the world go by, or stopping passing cars if there was the chance of a petty enquiry.

It was sufficiently calm late on the solstice day for English Heritage to open Stonehenge to the public – without the usual charge. There were no staff on duty to collect the admissions.

If the solstice was quiet, the autumn equinox was not – or so the County Council feared. Worried that the Convoy might materialize, the Council had holes dug for stout barriers to block off one of the green ways near Stonehenge. They were not big holes, but they were in a zone of archaeological sensitivity, and there was no archaeological supervision of their digging.

1990

Preliminaries for 1990 opened late in 1989 with English Heritage imposing the ban on Druids again.

As we go into 1990, then, the summer-solstice interest in Stonehenge keeps on popping up. To it is now added happenings at Stonehenge at each winter solstice, at the two equinoxes; before long, I am sure, Lammas, Beltane and who knows what other rediscovered pagan days will also be marked. And the practice has spread to Castlerigg and other prehistoric sites as well. In the course of normal professional visits to various sites all over Britain in the last year or two, I have noticed an increase, particularly at stone circles, in the amount of evidence, such as burnt areas and food debris, for recent use. These sites are coming into use again.

STONEHENGE AS A CURRENT AFFAIR

At one level the Stonehenge affair of the last 15 years, and particularly during the last five, can be viewed merely as a prolonged but nevertheless minor episode involving nothing more than an archaeological site, the anti-social behaviour of a few, ill-organized groups and the necessary steps taken by the authorities to deal with the nuisance. It would be fair to say that many do indeed see it, and would certainly like it kept, that way. But from a scholarly and practical interest in archaeology, and with my concern for the contemporaneity of the past, I see the affair as much more complex and dynamic – and consequently much more interesting. The events at Stonehenge harbour some 'real-world' issues that go some way towards explaining both the longevity and the passion of the affair.

Running through the affair are several themes. One is the extent of individual freedom in a democratic society; another is corporate responsibility in the public interest in a democratic society. Stonehenge is by no means unique, of course, in epitomizing such issues in contemporary society, but it is perhaps still a little surprising that a mere Ancient Monument should embrace them in such a public, and expensive, way. At first sight, Stonehenge hardly suggests itself as equivalent to such as Cheltenham GCHQ, Toxteth, the south Yorkshire coalfield, Wapping, the Rushdie affair or, more distantly, the mass trespass on Kinder; but in its recent role it has certainly at the very least overlapped the range of issues such episodes raised. Any surprise that such a role could be played by an archaeological site would, however, be a very English reaction. Elsewhere in the world, archaeological sites and material have been and are commonly at the forefront of public concern, usually centred around the basic question of who *owns* them.

Public Order, somewhat in doubt at moments during the affair, has plainly been restored. The mass gatherings have been stopped, the control of access to the Stones themselves has been very firmly asserted. To the relief of many, a democratically elected government and its agencies have not only repelled the real threat to law and order and to their very authority, but they have also successfully moved from a retaliatory stance to anticipatory action. The 'threat' in 1989 was not allowed to assemble, and indeed so visible was the official determination to prevent it that influential voices on the 'unofficial' side advised their followers not to set out for Stonehenge. Whether the benefit of this pro-active stance for public order justifies the consequential infringement, as some would see it, of civil liberties continues to be debated.

Over the years, the police role in the Stonehenge affair has been prominent, yet variable. No consistent policy has been followed as might have been expected had the powers-that-be seen Stonehenge each year as a matter of principle. Certainly the tactics have changed, perhaps as part of a strategy intended to cause uncertainty but actually giving the impression of year-to-year expediency. For years the police kept a 'watching brief only' at the Festival, then the reactionary violence of 1985 contrasted with the complete disengagement of 1988 and the pre-emptive ring-fence operation of 1989.

Hardly surprising, then, that such inconsistency has been interpreted as not really intended to prevent wrong-doing or even to keep the peace, but to harry a group in society which powers-that-be decided were obnoxious and meet to be expunged. That a million pounds or so can be spent each year in this hope seems even odder when contrasted with the refusal of all public bodies to spend a penny on a proper Festival site. A touch of financial comic relief, arising from the county lines that divide Police Authorities, has been the way in which the Convoy has been nudged across county boundaries so that another Constabulary could pick up the chase – and the bill.

A constant refrain within the variations on a police theme has been the costs to the public purse, and notably to Wiltshire rate-payers; an intermittent chord has queried the use and costs of private security firms and military forces. Impressive, in a way, though the raggle-taggle bob-tail of the assembling multitude has been, it simply has not matched, in any sense, the impressiveness at times of its own choosing of the co-ordinated display of official force. Indeed, on occasion it has been chilling, as presumably it was meant to be. Equally, given the opposition and judging it by the military criteria of the official forces, the latter have sometimes looked simply ludicrous. The well-advertised presence in one place at one time of many hundreds of police officers from several forces, with all their back-up of other police staff, vehicles, computers and helicopters, has also doubtless triggered idlers to wonder what the real criminals were simultaneously doing elsewhere.

The Stonehenge affair has highlighted the nature and needs of 'travelling people', bringing home the dichotomy between them and settled people as the realization dawned that the English had forgotten all about them. It needed to be explained – and was not – that nomads really do require a meeting place, not in any sense to be awkward or bloody-minded but from necessity. On the other hand, seekers after such places must accept that England's landscape is not a virgin Eden just waiting for them to do what they will wheresoever they choose, but a fairly complex product of 5000 years of man the farmer. In particular, it is a proprietorial palimpsest, all of it to all intents and purposes belonging to someone in a legal sense and, equally important, to others in a psychological or emotional sense. The Convoy transgressed legally by invading one farmer's field; it caused more dispersed but equally strong offence by camping in 'our' New Forest (an irony, since the present public access stems from its status as a Royal Forest, the likes of you and me as well as 'travellers' would have been excluded on pain of rather nasty punishment in medieval times).

Another theme, so far only implied, is the fascinating involvement and interrelationship of national bodies other than the Government and of local bodies other than the police. We can merely observe that this is an aspect of the Stonehenge affair which perhaps one day can be explored with appropriate documentation not available to us now. In particular, many have queried the roles of English Heritage, a quasi-independent but almost wholly Government-funded body created during the affair precisely to remove such matters from ministerial desks, and the National Trust, a wholly independent charity with

72 One of the Stonehenge freedoms is the right to take liberties with its image. Here Stonehenge is improved in an advert with a conservatory, pasted on a photomontage, over the slogan, 'We have just added a permanent feature.' Stonehenge is about 4000 years old. The company offer a 'no-quibble 10-Year Guarantee'.

statutory powers and obligations. Their attitudes have certainly raised questions about what they are protecting, for whom and from whom; and rather nastier questions in the minds of some about possible collusion not only with each other but with other interests too. Certainly, because of Stonehenge, the two bodies have had to act together more often and in ways which were not anticipated when possible future co-operation between the two bodies was discussed during the formative days of English Heritage.

The Forestry Commission, another statutory landowner, also became involved, and of course the ramifications through official and voluntary bodies at local level, from the County Councils downwards, became extensive and complex. In all this a number of matters would repay further study. Some involve obviously major decisions, for example to apply to the courts for injunctions banning individuals from the Stonehenge area and, in 1989, to create a *cordon sanitaire* around Stonehenge, in effect excluding everyone. But many other, apparently minor but actually crucial moments or events occurred in the field, moments such as that late on Friday 21 March 1986, when it became clear that nothing positive or practical was going to emerge from the great public meeting at Salisbury that day, or events such as the digging in 1985 of a deep trench across the entrance to the former Festival field.

Meanwhile, increasingly articulate groups see in Stonehenge, and other ancient sites, a powerful religiosity, alive and demanding certain observances. This is a fact, irrespective of the historical correctness or the validity of such beliefs, and it has implications about the functions now required of sites hitherto, and still, managed on behalf of society solely as monumental relics. Beyond the relatively straightforward religious beliefs is a further morass of mysticism, not a new phenomenon but one perhaps now stronger in the very irrationality of its appeal to a predominantly godless society. Though the 'green movement' is anything but irrational, the speed with which it has become a factor in everyday life over recent years suggests at the very least an intuitive communal sense that there are values other than material prosperity; and in a general way the different and vaguely religious views now being expressed of such well known monuments like Stonehenge are part of the same human sensitivity.

I do not personally see such a great divide in these matters as some have argued. It is common for many people to sense something special about the place when they visit ancient sites; indeed, that is part of their attraction. We go not just to see but also to feel, to try to experience something of what we imagine may well once have been. Even for the most travel-soaked tourist, there has to be some expectation, otherwise there is no point; and that expectation is likely to include elements of wonder and perhaps respect, possibly even reverence. Non-packaged individuals who choose the occasions for their visits certainly expect, and often receive, deeper vibes. So there is but a matter of degree across a broad range of potential human experience, not a fundamental distinction, in the feelings of a tourist, an academic, a geomancer, a Druid and a pagan mystic as each contemplates a stone circle. My own guess is that an elemental ancestor-worship is common to them all.

Stonehenge has been and is a catalyst; it will doubtless remain so, whether or not our society remains democratic. In a sense we marvel at its power to liberate such a complex and powerful array of forces, intellectual, emotional and physical; but in another, perhaps professional, sense, as long-term puzzlers over the Stonehenge phenomenon, we are not surprised at all. Its power to inspire is documented since medieval times; God knows what it did before then. Though we would not go quite all the way with the mystic and scholar John Michell, we find ourselves in the same parish when he writes: 'The matter of Stonehenge is not merely parochial. Whatever happens there is crucially important to the future of this country and may well determine the shape of things to come. . . .' Maybe elements of the future are glimpsed in the story of Stonehenge's recent past discussed in this chapter, and it is to this future that we now turn.

CHAPTER SEVEN

STONEHENGE
TOMORROW

Christopher Chippindale and Peter Fowler

THE NEW STONEHENGES

Stonehenge is a lively place nowadays, more lively than it has been for some generations. And building Stonehenges is becoming the fashion. Astonishingly, there are now six Stonehenges, more or less, in the world, five of them in north America, and four of them built in the 1980s. Two are stone, in Missouri and in Texas. The most recent are two henges made out of old cars, the Carhenge built in Alliance (Nebraska) by an oil engineer in 1987, and the Autohenge built near Lake Ontario by sculptor Bill Lishman in 1986 (fig. 73). The Autohenge is advertising art, commissioned by the Chrysler Corporation for a television commercial with the message that Chrysler cars 'are a giant step forward and everything else is history'. It is a splendid thing. Lishman partially crushed the cars in a scrap baler, and tied them in pairs with steel bands to get blocks of the right proportions. The site is superbly chosen; like Stonehenge it is neither on a mountain top nor in a valley bottom, but placed on a low knoll, complete with farm-track by way of processional avenue to approach the sacred place. From a distance its silhouette so well follows Stonehenge's that a photograph of the Autohenge against the setting sun fools most people. Close up the combination of ancient and grandiose shape with debased modern materials is startling.

The Autohenge, intended to be temporary, is happily to be left standing. So is Carhenge, after the Nebraska state planning authority was persuaded it was a sculpture, not a dump of scrap automobiles, and conformed to its zoning laws. The Autohenge is acquiring associations of its own as a place of ritual. In August 1987, mystics around the world celebrated the 'harmonic convergence' a special node in the motions of the world which stirred those whose lives sense the vibrations. In England harmonics converged on Glastonbury, as the right kind of ancient place to feel the forces; converging on Stonehenge would only cause more aggravation, and perhaps the oppression of police, military and private-security

73 King of the new henges is the Ontario Autohenge, seen from the air in afternoon light. Its designer, Bill Lishman, took trouble to follow the horseshoe plan of the English prototype.
Courtesy of Bill Lishman.

guards on the place are destroying its ancient aura. As Ontario is less supplied with ancient places of repute, the gathering there chose the Autohenge. And the plan for the 1990s is to celebrate each summer solstice with a rock festival round the Autohenge.

The older replica Stonehenges have their special roles too. The first that still stands, the concrete Stonehenge at Maryhill, by the Columbia river in Washington state, has become a gathering place for motorbike gangs, who find it the right kind of spot to carry out their own rituals.

One country which lacks a new Stonehenge is Britain. The real place has been closed to visitors for years now, and will probably have to stay that way. Which is why we need another Stonehenge, one that can be improved, tinkered with, climbed on, played with, and generally treated with less respect. It might be built of plastic mouldings. We would call it Foamhenge.

THE NEW STONEHENGES AND THE OLD
STONEHENGE

What does the Autohenge have to do with prehistoric Stonehenge. Not much. What does it tell us about prehistoric Stonehenge? Nothing whatever. It is a modern artefact; if it tells us about anything, it tells us about ourselves and what we today think of Stonehenge. The same is true of the Druids who meet at Stonehenge today and hold the place sacred. They are not historically authentic, and we have no grounds for believing that they really re-enact the religion and ritual of the builders of Stonehenge (though there have been would-be Druids for so long now, that these pretenders have themselves become an institution with a history).

It is said that one of the leading British enthusiasts for researching into the mystic powers of stone circles experiences, on entering a stone circle, an overwhelming urge to empty her bowels. This may be true; if it is, then it tells us more about her bowels than about the builders of the stone circles.

All this is perfectly harmless, as long as it is clear that these are modern responses to Stonehenge which tell us nothing about ancient Stonehenge. The sincerity with which the Druids hold to their beliefs is not the point, any more than the strength of emotion and spirit felt at the harmonic convergence around the (brand-new, and wholly secular) Autohenge.

The mischief comes when the modern responses are projected back in the hope or pretence that they relate to the realities of prehistory. This is not just a question that arises with the rock festivals, the Autohenges or the advertisement that builds a Stonehenge out of video recorders – the responses to Stonehenge that are obviously modern. It also arises with the Druids, who look vaguely antique and who appear to have been worshipping at Stonehenge since time immemorial (though in reality only this century). And it is certainly a question that arises with Stonehenge astronomy. One of the Stonehenge astronomers explained his methods in these terms: if I can see any relation, alignment or use for part of Stonehenge, then that relation, alignment or use was also known to its builders. It sounds an unexceptional statement, but what is one to make of the fact that Stonehenge, when the right series of calculations are applied, enables you to predict the date of Passover, or of Easter, or come to that, of next week's opening times at Sainsbury's?

This is why archaeologists, delighted that Stonehenge is still a living place today, dislike the confusion between ancient and modern that arises in thinking that the Druids really belong to Stonehenge, or in pretending that Stonehenge was an astronomical observatory in any proper sense. The particular role of archaeologists in knowing Stonehenge is to keep the things we really know about ancient Stonehenge distinct from the very different things we choose to make of Stonehenge today.

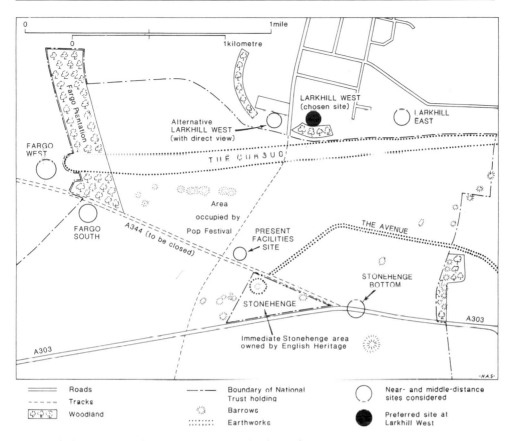

74 English Heritage plans to remove the facilities from immediately north-west of Stonehenge to a new Visitor Centre at a greater distance. This map sets out options that were seen in 1985. English Heritage was in 1989 able to secure the go-ahead for its preferred site, at Larkhill West.
Map by Arthur Shelley.

MANAGING THE MONUMENT

Whether or not Stonehenge further shapes the pattern of our lives, something has to be done about the monument, and its setting (fig. 74). Again, proposals involve questions of ownership and, beyond that, the matter of for whom is or should be the conservation and presentation of the site (fig. 75) and its surroundings to be carried out?

Here the divided legal ownership is central. The nation owns Stonehenge itself; on its behalf, the Secretary of State for the Environment legally owns it and he, through the National Heritage Act (1984), has vested its management as a Guardianship Monument in the Historic Buildings and Monuments Commission (English Heritage for short). With Stonehenge goes a little triangle of land only, an island within the National Trust's Stonehenge estate, which takes in most of the land around Stonehenge. All has been designated by the Trust 'inalienable', which means that, by an Act of Parliament, the Trust cannot dispose of its ownership and only Parliament can take it away. None of the Trust land is 'in hand'; all of it is leased to tenant-farmers. About 1½ km (1 mile) to the north is the southern edge of the Salisbury Plain Training Area, owned by the Ministry of Defence.

During 1987, the Trust opened 'Archaeological Walks' about its Stonehenge estate, a network of footpaths enabling – indeed encouraging – walkers to visit the burial mounds and other archaeological features in the Stonehenge landscape (fig. 76). It was intended not least to help people to see 'the Stones' in a topographical perspective and to spread the visitor pressure away from the monument itself. This welcome initiative, very much in accord with current archaeological thinking and tourist management practice, is possible because the Trust is the landowner and because a great deal of archaeological survey effort has been invested in the Stonehenge environs over the last decade by the Royal Commission on the Historical Monuments of England, English Heritage and the Wessex Archaeological Trust. The context of 'the Stones' is now much better documented and appreciated; a vastly-improved, and in significant respects different, background to Stonehenge now exists and will provide the basis also for the presentation of the area in a new Visitor Centre.

For years now, English Heritage has been trying to persuade the Ministry of

75 Until a new scheme is in place, the dismal design of the present facilities will continue as the foreground to Stonehenge, an eyesore unworthy of a temple. *Photograph by Christopher Chippindale.*

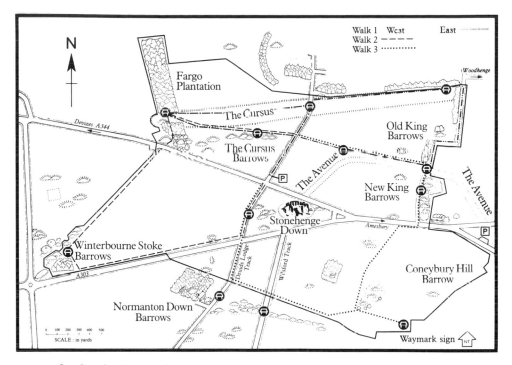

76 Leaflet for the National Trust walks around Stonehenge shows how visitors can explore the landscape and its many other monuments.
By courtesy of the National Trust.

Defence to provide land and access for the new Centre about 1½ km (1 mile) north of Stonehenge itself. All parties are agreed that the present visitor facilities are hopeless, too close, too cramped, too intrusive. Resisting the temptation to build a high-tech Centre and car-park underground, beneath the present surface car-park, English Heritage decided to set the Visitor Centre at a decent distance. They identified this northern site as the best; from it people would walk across the grass of the open downs to Stonehenge – to step over the landscape as its builders did, to see Stonehenge as its builders saw it, rising up from the earth on the skyline. On the way, the cursus will be crossed and barrows passed, showing how the great stone monument exists in a cultural landscape of related man-made structures. The existence of this landscape, still surviving fragmentarily, has led to the Stonehenge area, with Avebury, being recognized by UNESCO as a 'World Heritage Site' along with the Taj Mahal, the Great Pyramids, and Hadrian's Wall.

There is no provision for a permanent festival site in the current plans of the Trust or English Heritage.

In a number of different 'visions of the future' for Stonehenge, there seems general agreement that the immediate area must be cleared of visible modern intrusions, that the wider environs must be made more available to visitors; and that the A344 road, cutting the north edge of the henge and separating it from the Avenue, should be closed to through traffic. The idea of a new visitor centre away from the monument and out of sight is also widely approved.

Differences persist over detail – important detail. Local residents, understandably, oppose the closure of the A344 which is a most convenient local route. The busy A303 just to the south of Stonehenge, the trunk road from London to the south-west, is currently visually intrusive and noisy with its continuous heavy traffic. To bury the highway in a tunnel, or a deep cutting, would be expensive: is it worth £X million for non-essential engineering works to improve the Stonehenge experience for millions of people over the next years? We think so, for the dignity of the place, as well as to cheer the tourists. If visitors were invited to contribute a minimum of £1 towards this end, the cost would probably be raised voluntarily while the Department of Transport was still shuffling its papers on such a preposterous notion; cannot English Heritage and the National Trust start such a scheme, offering to match every pound so raised?

When it was first created, some years back, English Heritage bravely declared that the re-making of its Stonehenge arrangements would be a high priority. A fine plan was quickly developed; then there was a long silence, broken every six or nine months by discreet optimistic noises, but not by action. Apparently the military could not accept a visitor centre up at Larkhill, and the whole scheme was bogged down. Although every party dislikes the present arrangement, no consensus or means exists to achieve something better. The deadlock seems to us deeply unsatisfactory and terribly English.

The *impasse* seemed to have been broken in late 1989, when English Heritage announced that the Larkhill scheme could at last go ahead, with a £6 million visitor centre, a new access road to it from the east, and the closing of the A344. Local opinion was not pleased, and started a 'Save Stonehenge' scheme to block the plan. And English Heritage expected to have great difficulty financing the project, so it may well come again to nothing.

A few weeks later English Heritage announced a continuing ban on Druidic worship at Stonehenge, thus guaranteeing there will be trouble of some kind at the solstice of 1990, as is now the annual rite.

We make two further suggestions, the first entirely unoriginal.

We urge that a site for a Festival be found within a 16-km (10-mile) radius of Stonehenge. The site must definitely not be at or close to Stonehenge itself, but our understanding of what is needed, based on discussions with some of those involved, is a site within a few miles of 'the Stones'. By 'Festival site' we mean one with proper provision for catering for the needs of large numbers of people over short periods so that all legal and human requirements are met. And by 'Festival' we mean an occasion properly licensed with and approved by the appropriate authorities. The precedents lie not only with the private-sector arrangements for large open-air festivals and pop-concerts at Glastonbury or Knebworth but also at the major, permanent showgrounds for the great agricultural shows like that of the Bath and West at Shepton Mallet. Indeed, a multi-purpose site could become a mecca for Wessex rather than just a once-a-year Stonehenge Festival site. And, as the present political climate requires, the funding of such a development would be entirely appropriate through a mixture of both private and public monies.

A STONEHENGE MANAGER

Our other suggestion, lower level and pragmatic, we think to be crucial. Stonehenge must have its own manager; someone, an individual, who is responsible directly for it, bringing to it professionalism and also, we would hope, care through pride in a unique post. The present situation is hopeless: the splendid chaps on site are site custodians, within an hierarchical organization influenced by its Civil Service origins, and very near the bottom of the institutional pecking order. Their 'line manager' – and how often does that mean in practice a 'telephone-line manager'? – is an Inspector of Ancient Monuments, operating out of London, covering a large area of southern England, and weighed down with dozens of files all demanding action about other Properties in Care. This is no way to look after the real needs of a World Heritage Site – one of the great structures of prehistoric Europe, Britain's greatest megalithic site – and now, in all those guises and many another, enmeshed in many a complex situation. Just as a business, Stonehenge has a turnover of several hundred thousand pounds a year and a most conspicuous public profile. It needs someone who is there *and* very much in charge. Similarly, although the National Trust responsibilities are fitted into the operations of the regional staff from their headquarters at Stourhead, no one of sufficient seniority either has Stonehenge as his major or sole responsibility or is actually *there* most of the time, actually on the spot. The need for a senior 'Stonehenge manager', working on the site and living locally is self-evident (a similar post was recently created for Hampton Court). The Trust and English Heritage should consider a joint post, or some other mechanism, so that an integrated approach to the management of the monument in its setting becomes the norm, in place of the disjointed crisis management which has characterized the last decade.

A 'Stonehenge and Environs Manager', concentrating on his or her 'patch' without other responsibilities, would know it in a way which others operating from offices elsewhere cannot. This could improve the consideration given to knotty, practical, on-site problems such as access, the amount and nature of fencing in the area, and the landscape around the monument (fig. 77). At present, the triangle of grass around it between the two main roads and a track to the west

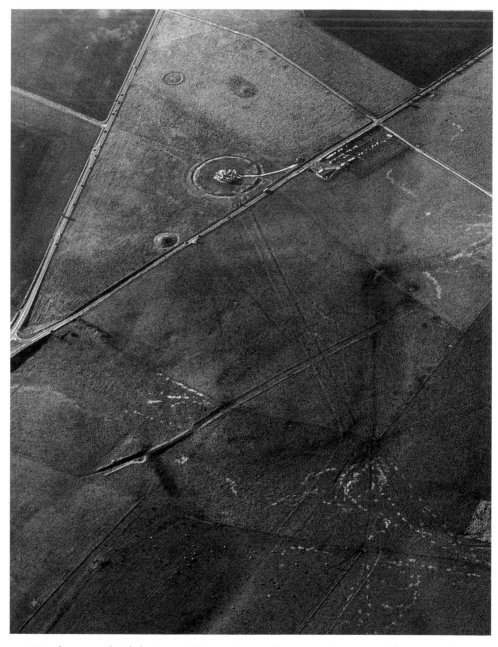

77 Air photograph of the immediate environs shows a palimpsest of features of different dates.

The faint double line running down from Stonehenge (centre, near top) is the Avenue, the prehistoric ceremonial way to Stonehenge. In mid picture it crosses a more prominent, diagonal earthwork, believed to be an eighteenth-century turnpike road, abandoned in mid construction.

is virtually an island in a sea of arable. While there is a case for restoring the 'traditional' downland turf over a wider area, it is not a wholly simple matter.

In the first place, assuming the National Trust accepted the idea, its tenant farmers would have to agree to changes in leases or to accept new terms when leases came up for renewal. In return for imposing a less 'commercial' way of farming, the Trust would have to be prepared to accept lower rents – or so the argument has run. Now that the economics of European agriculture are changing fundamentally, a constraint on the amount of land under arable should be less of a financial handicap than was once supposed. Nevertheless, the Trust and its tenants operate in the real world of farm prices; just as the tenants would not wish to see the profitability of their work reduced, so the Trust would not enjoy the thought of lower rents when its income from this source is already threatened by declining farming values.

If any area in Britain is deliberately to be taken out of cultivation to reduce the national production of cereal, then surely the land around Stonehenge must be one of the most readily justifiable priorities: it is one of the most outstanding prehistoric landscapes of Europe, indeed in the world, according to its 'World Heritage' status. The move would cost money; but surely not just the Trust's. And the gain would be far more than just visual. The restitution of a sheep-grazed, flora-rich herbage would encourage faunal species to re-colonize their natural habitat. What price great bustards over Stonehenge again, as on Loggan's seventeenth-century engraving?

But the swelling downland landscape of close-cropped grass is itself an artefact, made through the ages by man the tree-feller and his domesticated animals, not a 'natural' thing. If we wish to change the present landscape back, to what do we return it? To the post-glacial forest or to the view contemporary with Stonehenge? And if so, contemporary with which Stonehenge? – the structure of 2500 BC, of 2000 BC, or of 1500 BC? Or do we reconstitute a medieval landscape, or one of the ones depicted by the seventeenth-, eighteenth- or nineteenth-century topographers and artists, or that of the early twentieth century which is recoverable from OS maps and photographs, including early air photographs?

Stonehenge's surroundings, always changing, have looked different from time to time; in trying to restore, or re-create, a past landscape we first have to be clear in our own minds what we are trying to do, and for whom. The clumps of trees, often on barrows, such a marked feature of the much-loved 'traditional' downland landscape, result from deliberate planting mostly in the earlier nineteenth century; they have no place in Stonehenge's ancient landscape. Do we remove them? Probably not, since they are so 'traditional'. If they stay, do we also leave the later plantations of conifers, which many find more 'alien', less 'in keeping'. Part of Fargo plantation, one of those coniferous plantations, has already been taken out, the better to conserve the earthworks it runs over. Where is the logic, the true historical validity, in this? Once we start tampering in the name of 'restoration' with something as complex as the landscape, sentiment and prejudice, perhaps unconsciously, are as likely to determine the product as reason and research.

In all these deliberations is a question, not so much 'Who owns Stonehenge?' as 'Who is Stonehenge to be for?' Not exclusively for archaeologists, of that we can be certain; though we give them a special responsibility for the well-being of the surviving evidence and the presentation of its nature and significance to non-specialists, in the same way that it is astronomers rather than astrologers who study and professionally watch the presentation of our knowledge of the stars. But Stonehenge should not, and ultimately cannot, belong to any one minority – and that includes tourists who, though by far the largest group of 'users' in any one year, are still a small fraction of Stonehenge's varied audience (fig. 78) on a world stage over the centuries. In the coming years tourist-led demands, particularly given English Heritage's statutory brief and commercial pressures, could tilt management and presentation policies towards populist solutions. Inevitably, any constraints in access or higher than low-brow tones in presentation will be charged as 'elitist' but if ever an ancient site with landscape

78 *Christmashenge*; watercolour by Mervyn Grist in pastiche of a medieval manuscript illumination of the wizard Merlin building Stonehenge.
Christmas card for the county council library service, 1989; by courtesy of Wiltshire County Council.

was 'élite' it is Stonehenge. In the end, the best way of helping people to appreciate its 'specialness' is to treat it as something special.

That said, we believe access should be as open as is consonant with bearable wear and tear on the site; and, whatever the details of management and conservation practice, above all Stonehenge should have a sense of being restored to the people. They own it, legally by the terms of its gift to the British nation, and spiritually as a part of mankind's inheritance. It needs looking after, a highly professional, skilled management task; but, here, the best sort of management is invisible, enabling each of the annual tens of thousands of visitors to make his or her own discovery and to find an individual significance. There really is no place on the Stonehenge scene for barriers, turnstiles, proprietor's notices or men in uniform – of any sort. It is a place for quiet sensitivity, style and taste, an occasional beano perhaps and a little fun and games; but very definitely not as a backdrop for ostentatious PR, busy officialdom or information imperialism. The visitor must feel able to come to the monument as he will.

That we and many others feel strongly about Stonehenge is witness to its power. We sense that we, along with anybody else interested, own Stonehenge, individually in a way but more importantly in a collective sense, yet there really can be only one answer to our question: 'Who owns Stonehenge?' – 'No one.'

In arriving at that conclusion rather than the more obvious 'Stonehenge belongs to everyone', we wonder whether we have asked the right question. During the brief years of this book's gestation, 1986–9, human perception of the human condition has subtly but profoundly changed, at least in the Western world. A pre-occupation with an ethic of possession looks short-sighted on a globe threatened with environmental and ecological change, possibly disaster, in addition to nuclear oblivion. In that perspective, which more of us seem now to glimpse, arguments about who owns this or that begin to pale into insignificance. Indeed, the whole concept of personal or corporate proprietorship may well change, and even be weakened by a growing irrelevance. What is the point of owning something, or making the effort of acquisition, if your environment cannot sustain your life?

Has our question been overtaken by events while we were attempting to answer it? There may be a terrible truth in our answer, 'No one'. No one may be around to own a non-existent monument by the mid thirtieth century on an inundated, overheated globe; but long before then, we suspect, the question will have become unanswerable because, sociologically, psychologically, conceptually, it will have become impossible to ask it. Stonehenge is 40 and more centuries old; it has seen more than anyone of us ever has; and it may yet outlive us all, even humanity itself.

FURTHER READING

We set down here suggestions for readers who might want to explore further the themes of this book.

There are competent guidebooks with colour illustrations available at Stonehenge. The site is just west of Amesbury, Wiltshire. It is in the care of English Heritage, which opens it daily; admission is free to National Trust members.

R. J. C. Atkinson, *Stonehenge* (London: Hamish Hamilton, 1956; and reprinted with a little revision in Pelican paperback), though old, is still the clearest description of just what there is at Stonehenge, together with an archaeological interpretation which is no longer up-to-date. A much older study, William Long's *Stonehenge and Its Barrows* (Devizes: Wiltshire Archaeological & Natural History Society, 1876), remains useful.

There are two books on the later history of Stonehenge, that is, on the re-discovery of the site and what has been made with it and of it over the centuries: Michael Balfour, *Stonehenge and Its Mysteries* (London: Macdonald & Jane's, 1979); and Christopher Chippindale, *Stonehenge Complete* (London: Thames & Hudson, 1983).

No collected account of events at Stonehenge in the 1980s exists, beyond the one in this book, but there are partial stories in a pamphlet: John Michell, *Stonehenge: Its Druids, Custodians, Festival and Future* (London: Radical-Traditionalist Press, 2nd edition, 1987); and in an academic-journal paper: Christopher Chippindale, 'Stoned Henge: events and issues at the summer solstice', *World Archaeology* 18 (1986): 38–58. The NCCL booklet *Stonehenge: a Report into the Civil Liberties Implications of the Events Relating to the Convoys of Summer 1985 and 1986* (London: NCCL, 1986) examines what its title says.

The theme of 'Who owns the past?', is explored in the essays of a book of that title: Isobel MacBryde, *Who Owns the Past?* (Melbourne: Oxford University Press, 1985; and in Oxford Paperbacks); and runs through David Lowenthal, *The Past is a Foreign Country* (Cambridge: Cambridge University Press, 1985).

Alfred Watkins's *The Old Straight Track* (London: Methuen, 1925; and Abacus paperback) is the original ley classic; and later, Paul Devereux and Ian Thomson, *The Ley-Hunter's Companion* (London: Thames & Hudson, 1979; currently available in digest form as *The Ley Guide*, Penzance, Empress, 1977). Don Robins, *Circles of Silence* (London: Souvenir, 1985) and Paul Devereux, *Places of Power*, (London: Blandford, 1990) set out the phenomena surrounding the stone circles. Nigel Pennick & Paul Devereux, *Lines on the Landscape: Leys and Other Linear Enigmas* (London: Robert Hale, 1989) is a new summary of the field. *The Ley-Hunter* (PO Box 92, Penzance, Cornwall, UK) is the key periodical.

The story of the Welsh revival is set out at book length by Prys Morgan and David Thomas, *Wales: the Shaping of a Nation* (Newton Abbot: David & Charles, 1981), and more briefly in Morgan's essay in Eric Hobsbawm & Terence Ranger (ed.), *The Invention of Tradition* (Cambridge: Cambridge University Press, 1983). Stuart Piggott, *The Druids* (London: Thames & Hudson, 1968; and Pelican paperback) is an archaeologist's and historian's study of the Druids in reality and imagination.

John Michell's books, such as *City of Revelation* (London: Garnstone, 1972) and *The New View over Atlantis* (London: Thames & Hudson, 1983), make a good introduction to the Druid vision.

For the archaeological view of Stonehenge, there is R. J. C. Atkinson, *Stonehenge*; and Aubrey Burl, *The People of Stonehenge* (London: Dent, 1987), with vivid interpretation of the meaning of the site. L. V. Grinsell, *Legendary History and Folklore of Stonehenge* (St Peter Port, Guernsey: Toucan Press, 1975), is a thorough compilation of other interpretations. The archaeology of the monuments in the immediate area is surveyed in a report by the Royal Commission for the Historical Monuments (England): *Stonehenge and its Environs: Monuments and Land Use* (Edinburgh: Edinburgh University Press, 1979); and attractively summarized in Julian Richards's little booklet *Beyond Stonehenge* (Salisbury: Trust for Wessex Archaeology, 1985). Caroline Malone, *Avebury* (London: English Heritage/B. T. Batsford, 1989) is a good guide to the other great prehistoric complex in Wiltshire. Timothy Darvill, *Prehistoric Britain* (London: Batsford, 1987) is a first-rate introduction to current archaeological views of the larger background.

REFERENCES

Chapter One

1 Aubrey Burl, *The Stonehenge People* (London: Dent, 1987), p. 172.

2 Wiliam Stukeley, *Stonehenge* (London, 1740).

3 Gerald Hawkins and John B. White, *Stonehenge Decoded* (London: Souvenir, 1966).

4 But see Christopher Chippindale, 'Stonehenge Astronomy: anatomy of a modern myth', *Archaeology*, January-February 1986, pp. 48-52.

5 John Michell, *A Little History of Astro-archaeology: Stages in the Transformation of a Heresy* (London: Thames & Hudson, 1977), pages 5-6.

6 I give the same advice: go early or late, preferably in winter, preferably during the week, preferably in the sort of weather that would discourage anyone else.

7 About one visitor in three at Stonehenge is from north America. Not understanding fully the cultural meaning of Boca Raton, I consulted an American colleague; she explained, 'It's a place in Florida where people who wish they were like Richard Nixon retire to.'

8 Christopher Chippindale, 'What future for Stonehenge', *Antiquity* 57 (1983): 172-80.

Chapter Two

1 Ernest J. Eitel, *Feng Shui* (1873). London: Synergetic Press, 1984.

2 Nigel Pennick, *Hitler's Secret Sciences*. London: Neville Spearman, 1981.

3 George Eogan, *Knowth*. London: Thames & Hudson, 1986.

4 Martin Brennan, *The Stars and the Stones*. London: Thames & Hudson, 1983.

5 John A. Glover, 'Paths of shadow and light', *The Ley Hunter* 87 (1979).

6 A. Thom, 'Glastonbury as a possible megalithic observatory', in *A Study in Patterns*. London: Research Into Lost Knowledge Organisation, 1970.

7 PO Box 92, Penzance, Cornwall,

TR18 2XL, UK.

8 A. Thom, *Megalithic Sites in Britain*. Oxford: Oxford University Press, 1967. Gerald Hawkins & John B. White, *Stonehenge Decoded*. London: Souvenir, 1965. E. C. Krupp (ed.), *In Search of Ancient Astronomies*. New York: Doubleday, 1977. E. C. Krupp (ed.), *Echoes of the Ancient Skies*. New York: Harper & Row, 1983. John Michell, *A Little History of Astro-Archaeology*. London: Thames & Hudson, 1977. Euan W. MacKie, *Science and Society in Prehistoric Britain*. London: Elek, 1977. Douglas C. Heggie, *Megalithic Science*. London: Thames & Hudson, 1981.

9 Alfred Watkins, *Ancient British Trackways*. London: Simpkin &

Marshall, 1922. Alfred Watkins, *The Old Straight Track*. 1925. London: Garnstone Press, 1970. Alfred Watkins, *The Ley-hunter's Manual*. 1927. London: Pentacle, 1977. Alfred Watkins, *Archaic Tracks around Cambridge*. 1932.

10 Jonathan Mullard, 'Over Old Ground', *The Ley Hunter* 100 (1986).

11 Maria Reiche, *Peruvian Ground Drawings*. Munich: Kunstraum Munchen, 1974.

12 Tony Morrison, *Pathways to the Gods*. Michael Russell, 1978.

13 Tony Morrison, presentation at *The Ley Hunter* Moot, York, 1985.

14 Chris Kincaid (ed.), *Chaco Roads Project, Phase I*. US Bureau of Land Management, 1983.

15 John Michell, *The Old Stones of Land's End*. London: Garnstone, 1974.

16 Paul Devereux & Ian Thomson, *The Ley Hunter's Companion*. London: Thames & Hudson, 1979. (Revised as *The Ley Guide*. Empress, 1987.)

17 Glyn Daniel, *Megaliths in History*. London: Thames & Hudson, 1972.

18 Paul Devereux & Ian Thomson, *The Ley Hunter's Companion*. London: Thames & Hudson, 1979.

19 Tom Williamson & Liz Bellamy, *Ley Lines in Question*. Tadworth: World's Work, 1983.

20 Nigel Pennick & Paul Devereux, *Lines on the Landscape*. London: Robert Hale, 1989.

21 R. J. C. Atkinson, *Stonehenge*. 1956. Harmondsworth: Penguin, 1979.

22 J. F. S. Stone, 'The Stonehenge Cursus and its affinities', *Archaeological Journal* (1947).

23 Patricia M. Christie, The Stonehenge Cursus, *Wiltshire Archaeological & Natural History Magazine* 58 (1963).

24 Brian Larkman, 'The York ley', *The Ley Hunter* 100 (1986). Nigel Pennick, *Landscape Lines, Leys and Limits in Old England*. Cambridge: Runestaff, 1987.

25 John Michell, *Ancient Metrology*.

Bristol: Pentacle, 1981.

26 Geoffrey of Monmouth, *The History of the Kings of Britain* [c. 1136]. Harmondsworth: Penguin, 1966.

27 Leslie V. Grinsell, *Folklore of Prehistoric Sites in Britain*. Newton Abbot: David & Charles, 1976. Janet & Colin Bord, *The Secret Country*. London: Elek, 1976.

28 The Dragon Project Trust, c/o Empress, PO Box 92, Penzance, Cornwall, TR18 2XL, UK.

29 Francis Hitching, *Earth Magic*. London: Cassell, 1976. Charles Brooker, 'Magnetism and the Standing Stones', *New Scientist*, 13 January 1983. Don Robins, 'The Dragon Project and the Talking Stones', *New Scientist*, 21 October 1982. Paul Devereux, Operation Merlin, *The Ley Hunter* 88 (1980). Paul Devereux, 'An Ear to the Ground', *The Unexplained* 80. London: Orbis, 1982. Don Robins, *Circles of Silence*. London: Souvenir, 1985. Marco Bischof, 'Das Magische ist Messbar', *Esotera*, April 1987. Paul Devereux, *Places of Power*. London: Blandford, 1990.

30 Robin Baker, *The Mystery of Migration*. London: Macdonald Futura, 1985.

31 John Downer, *Supersense*. 1973. London: BBC Books, 1974. Guy Lyon Playfair & Scott Hill, *The Cycles of Heaven*. 1978. New York: Avon, 1979.

32 Pierre Méreaux, *Carnac – une Porte vers l'Inconnu*. Paris: Laffont, 1981.

33 Paul Devereux, *Earth Lights*. Wellingborough: Turnstone, 1982. Michael A. Persinger & Gyslaine Lafrenière, *Space-time Transients*. Nelson-Hall, 1977. Paul Devereux, Paul MacCartney & Don Robins, 'Bringing UFOs down to earth', *New Scientists*, 1 September 1983. John S. Derr, 'Luminous Phenomena and their Relationship to Rock Fracture', *Nature*, 29 May 1986. Paul Devereux, *Earth Lights Revelation*. London: Blandford, 1989. Brian T. Brady & Glen A. Rowell, *Nature*, 29 May 1986.

INDEX OF NAMES